GUIDE TO PENSIONS

GW00725513

ROSTERS LTD

GUIDE TO PENSIONS

Jenny Harris
and
Rosemary Burr

ROSTERS LTD

Published by ROSTERS LTD
23 Welbeck St, London, W1M 7PG

© Rosters Ltd
ISBN 1-85631-023-X

Published in the UK by ROSTERS
Typeset by County Typesetters, Margate, Kent
Printed and bound in Great Britain by Cox and Wyman Ltd, Reading

First edition 1991

PREFACE

I am pleased to introduce the Sun Life Guide to Pensions. Most of us will spend more than a quarter of our lives retired; preparing financially can be a daunting task. This book explores the whole range of pensions, from the basic state scheme to executive plans. In it, you'll find out more about bridging the gap between the world of work and a life of leisure. You have many choices as you plan for the future. I hope you will find this book an essential guide to understanding them.

John Reeve
Managing Director
Sun Life Assurance Society plc.

ACKNOWLEDGEMENTS

With thanks to everyone at Sun Life Assurance who worked on the project, in particular John Kirkhope, Liz Christie and Eddie O'Regan. Also, to Alison Leach.

About Sun Life

Sun Life is one of the UK's leading financial services organisations. Founded in 1810, we opened our first offices directly opposite the Bank of England – we have always been at the centre of events. Throughout the 180 years of our existence, we have sought to provide the highest quality products and services. It is a reputation we are proud of and you can be sure of. Today we manage approximately £9 billion to meet the needs of over 1 million customers. We're growing from strength to strength.

CONTENTS

INTRODUCTION:
TAX-FREE RETIREMENT
PLANNING

If you were offered two apples of exactly the same size and variety but one cost 25p and the other 50p which would you choose? Obviously the one which cost 25p. You may think this is a silly question but, when it comes to investment, many people are turning down the chance to buy their savings in the cheapest possible manner; they are doing the equivalent of buying apples at 50p which are also on sale for 25p. Of course they don't realise that this is what they are doing, as few of us know the real costs of the investments we make. All too often we concentrate on considering what we actually wish to invest in, shares or property for example, rather than the way we wish to invest, such as direct, via a unit trust, life policy or pension. However, your return on any savings product is not just influenced by the underlying investment itself but also by tax and charges. What is important for you to know is the actual return on your savings after tax.

In terms of after-tax return, pensions win hands down. You receive tax relief on your savings, they grow tax free inside the plan and you normally have the option of taking a tax-free lump sum on retirement. Despite these tax incentives, it seems that one person in three of the working population ignores this form of saving and simply relies on the state to provide them with an income once they have retired.

You only have to compare the figures for average weekly earnings and the state pension to see how short-sighted such a strategy is when it comes to trying to plan for a prosperous retirement. In 1990 the average gross weekly earnings for men were £295.60 and for women £201.50, yet the basic state pension for those who had paid the necessary National Insurance contributions throughout the majority of their working life is a mere £52.00 per week in 1991/92. You may also qualify for some State Earnings Related Pension (SERPS) if you have paid full National Insurance contributions, but even this additional income will not make up the difference between earnings and state pension. What is worse, the government is reducing the sums it will pay through the state earnings scheme in the future. Also, this scheme is not available for the self-employed. So the message is clear – the state will not provide you with a pension which will maintain your standard of living when you have retired.

However, there is no need to despair. Recent changes in pension legislation have made it easier for people to take charge of their own retirement planning and have given them a more flexible vehicle for doing so in the form of personal pensions, which are actually portable investment plans you can take from job to job. With this new freedom to choose your own pension comes a series of difficult choices. You are no longer tied to your company pension, but should you stay in it or go solo? If you decide to do your own thing, what pension should you choose? Planning for your retirement is a very individual matter and, before you take the step of picking a pension, it pays to do plenty of homework. In order to get the best out of your pension you have to be clear not only about your current financial situation and needs but also about your requirements for the future. For example, if like many people you may want to retire before the statutory retirement age (sixty-five for men, sixty for women) then you need to consider this at the outset and ensure you will not be penalised for such an option and that the plan is properly funded to give you this flexibility.

In this book we take you step-by-step through the pensions maze and show you which key points you need to consider along the way in order to make the most of your pension planning. We also provide a detailed glossary of terms so that you can decipher the fine print and 'technospeak' which you may encounter when seeking advice or doing your own research.

We start by looking at how you should go about planning your pension whatever age bracket you are in. In Chapter Two we look at what the state can provide and give further details to show what sort of gap in earnings this will create for those who retire without making any extra provision of their own. Having identified the shortfall, we outline the options you face when choosing to top-up the state payment.

In Chapter Three we show you how to analyse the nuts and bolts of a company pension and where to get information on the particular scheme you may be offered. Chapter Four provides an over-view on personal pensions, including the choices available, the facilities which may be offered and a checklist to help you choose the most suitable product for your needs. Chapter Five gives advice on making the best choice of pension product to meet your needs. In Chapter Six we take a close look at pension planning for executives, the choices open to them and how to judge which would be the most suitable option for you.

Finally, in Chapter Seven we show how you can reap

maximum benefit from your assiduous savings and planning. We look at the implications of when you choose to retire and draw your pension on the sum of money you will have to provide you with a retirement income for life. Also, we examine the factors you should consider when deciding whether to draw the maximum lump sum from your pension or to concentrate on generating income.

Throughout the book we highlight the tax implications of each choice based on current legislation. However, you do need to be aware that pensions are an area of some contention which could be affected by a change of government.

Pension planning is simple in theory but complex in reality! Each individual has different requirements and earnings patterns and each company sells slightly different savings plans. It is especially important to keep in mind these three basic principles:

- The longer your money is invested, the bigger your potential pension
- If you choose a personal pension then the ultimate size of your savings will depend on how good the company managing your money is at investing it on your behalf
- You pay for extra flexibility and facilities by receiving a lower pension, so you need to be clear which factors are important to you and which you do not need

This book cannot provide a tailor-made pension plan for each reader, but we hope we have given you the necessary tools to develop a successful retirement strategy and sufficient information to ensure that you are able to get the most benefit from professional advice.

CHAPTER ONE:
PENSION PLANNING

A good start to pension planning is to ask three simple questions. How much income will you need when you retire? If you do nothing, how much income will you actually have when you retire? If you will not have sufficient income, how can you make up the shortfall?

The first question is usually the easiest to answer but it still needs careful consideration. Partly, it comes down to age because if you are twenty-something, your financial needs in retirement will be less obvious than if you are fifty-something. If you are in your early twenties, you have probably only recently accepted the idea of planning for retirement and have no idea how much money you will need. If you are in your thirties, weighed down with responsibilities, then you probably have a more precise idea of how much you need to finance your current lifestyle and you can adjust this slightly to compensate for money spent on a growing family. By the time you are forty-something, if you have children, the costs should peak and you should be looking forward to an improved lifestyle when your children become financially independent. By the time you are fifty-something, your future financial needs should be easier to quantify with precision. However, whatever age you are, you need to take into account certain basic principles. In this chapter, we will look first at the fundamentals of pension planning and then at suitable strategies for the various age groups.

You may come across phrases or terms which are unfamiliar. Don't worry, many are covered in the Glossary and all are explained in the chapters which follow.

How much pension will you need?
It is generally accepted that most people will need a pension equal to two-thirds of their final salary at retirement in order to maintain their lifestyle. However, it is difficult to generalise as this obviously depends on your individual circumstances. It is sensible to begin with a personal audit of income and expenditure in order to establish how much pension you would need to maintain your present lifestyle and any adjustments you may require in the future. Although it is probably impossible to fill in such an audit completely accurately, it will give you a pretty good idea of how you would stand.

— *Out*
Items that can usually be deleted include: mortgage, because that will generally have been paid off by retirement; fares to work; private education; endowment policy premiums, if the policies mature at retirement; National Insurance; pension contributions.

— *Down*
Items that will normally be reduced include: holidays for the children; expenses for the car (unless you have run a company car).

— *Up*

Items that will increase will often include: the car, if you have used a company car for work; heating and lighting, because you will probably spend more time at home; hobbies, because you will have more time to enjoy yourself.

After you have made the necessary adjustments let's assume that you have come to the total of two-thirds final salary. You therefore need to check what you may be earning when you retire.

Table A: **RETIREMENT EARNINGS**

How much will you be earning at retirement, assuming your salary increases at 8% p.a.?

Current Salary (£000s)	Salary in 10 years (£000s)	Salary in 15 years (£000s)	Salary in 20 years (£000s)	Salary in 25 years (£000s)	Salary in 30 years (£000s)	Salary in 35 years (£000s)	Salary in 40 years (£000s)	Salary in 45 years (£000s)
10	21.5	31.7	46.6	68.4	100.6	147.8	217.2	319.2
15	32.3	47.5	69.9	102.7	150.9	221.7	325.8	478.8
20	43.1	63.4	93.2	136.9	201.2	295.7	434.5	638.4
25	53.7	79.3	106.6	171.1	251.5	369.6	543.1	798.0
30	64.5	95.1	139.8	205.4	301.8	443.5	651.7	957.6
35	75.5	111.0	163.1	239.6	352.2	517.4	760.3	1,117.2
40	86.3	126.8	186.6	373.9	402.5	591.4	869.0	1,276.8
45	95.8	142.7	209.7	408.1	452.8	665.3	997.2	1,436.4

From Table A you can see that if your salary is £10,000 a year now, your salary will be £21,500 in ten years' time if you get annual increases of 8% and that it will rise to £319,000 a year in forty-five years' time, if it increases at the same rate. Of course it is unlikely that your salary will rise by exactly 8% each year, but this is a rough estimate to give you some idea on what basis to do your calculation.

To work out what all this means in terms of pension provision is another matter and in Chapter Seven we will go more closely into the question of annuities, which are generally incomes for life. For the moment, however, let's use the nicely rounded rule of thumb measurement, based on the assumption that a 10% annuity will be available and adequate. This means that for every £1,000 of gross annual income you will want in retirement you will need a pension fund of £10,000.

Example A:
Juliet George, who has a personal pension fund of £150,000, is due to retire in ten years' time. She reckons that after receiving her basic state pension she will need an annual income of £15,000 at today's prices. She expects that inflation will average 8% a year. How much will she need in her pension fund in ten years' time?

The table shows that her required income will be £32,200. Multiply that by ten and you discover she will need a pension fund totalling £322,000. However, Juliet does not have to invest any more to achieve this. If she is prepared to gamble that her fund will grow at 8.5% p.a. (a fairly prudent amount), her final pension fund will be about £340,000. If it grows at 13% p.a. her fund will be significantly larger – £509,000.

Example B:
William Osborn is due to retire in ten years, by then having put in twenty years with his company which runs a 1/60th final salary scheme. This means his pension will be 20/60ths (one-third) of final salary. His salary is currently £30,000. Therefore he knows that whatever his final salary is, he will get one-third – that is £10,000 at today's prices – because that part of his pension will

18

increase in line with his earnings. However, if he wants a retirement income based on a full two-thirds final salary, he has to calculate the additional pension he needs to add the extra one-third to his retirement income.

William has to start by calculating what the extra £10,000 will be worth in ten years' time. Table A shows that it will be £21,500 if his earnings increase at 8% a year. Therefore, assuming that he expects to get a 10% annuity, he needs to build up a separate fund of £215,000 over the next ten years. He can do this by paying additional voluntary contributions.

If he assumes that his fund will grow at 8.5% p.a., he would need to invest an extra £170 per month for the next ten years to make up the shortfall. However, if he is more optimistic and assumes a growth of 13% p.a., he need only invest about £78 a month.

How much pension have you already got in the bag?
Your retirement income will be based on any pensions that you have qualified for under the state scheme with your current and previous employers, any personal pension or self-employed pension you have built up and any savings you have. You will need to establish how much you can expect to receive from each source.

— *State pensions*
There are two main state pension schemes. These are the basic state pension and the State Earnings Related Pension Scheme (SERPS). In Chapter Two we explain how each works and how your local office of the Department of Social Security can provide you with information about your state benefits on retirement.

At the present time, under normal circumstances, a married couple can expect a basic state pension of £52 a week (£2,704 p.a.) plus £31.25 (£1,625) additional pension for married women. If, however, both spouses qualify for a full basic state pension in their own right, they will not get the additional married woman's pension. A married couple will receive whichever combination gives them the largest income. If the wife, for example, has not qualified for a full basic pension, but has qualified for a pension in excess of the married woman's additional pension of £31.25 a week (£1,625 p.a.), then she will draw that instead of the married woman's pension. When making long term plans you can assume the basic pension to remain fairly constant because historically, regardless of the political complexion of the government, it is reasonably inflation-proofed and usually about 20% of the national average wage.

You may also be eligible for some State Earnings Related Pension Scheme (SERPS) payments. However, not everyone is entitled to this as sometimes a company pension scheme will opt out of SERPS. Individuals may also choose to opt out of SERPS.

— *Company pensions*
If you are in a company pension scheme, the scheme administrators should send you an annual statement telling you how much pension you have accumulated so far and how much you will receive if you stay in the scheme until normal retirement age.

If you are in a final salary scheme you can make your own estimate, provided you have a copy of the company scheme rule book which will explain the finer points. Chapter Three shows how you can calculate this figure for yourself. As final salary benefits are tied to the salary you receive when you retire, your ultimate pension is reasonably predictable – it is quantified in relation to your earnings. How much that will be in pounds and pence is less important if you are going to qualify for a full two-thirds final salary. However, you will get into difficulties if you cannot put in enough time to qualify for a full two-thirds pension and need to top it up with another pension, or if you are in a money purchase scheme or a personal pension where the ultimate value of your pension fund is linked to the investment return on your contributions.

— Personal pensions, money purchase schemes and AVCs

If you are in a money purchase scheme or a personal pension scheme your last statement from the pension provider will tell you how much money you have built up in your fund. The annuity table, Table G (page 69) explains how to estimate the amount of pension your fund will provide. You could also use this table to estimate how much income your retirement savings could generate if necessary.

— Previous employments

During your working life you may have had a number of jobs. If so, it could be a good idea to track down any pension rights from past employers (if they ran final salary schemes) and to consider getting them transferred to your own personal pension, or a buy-out plan. This will give you more control over your pension planning and could save you the heartbreak of seeing your pension rights from previous employers eroded by inflation. You can usually only do this if you were in a company pension scheme for at least two years (five years before 1988), but you may be pleasantly surprised at how much you have accumulated. If you were in company money purchase schemes the funds should continue to grow, so it may not be so urgent that you take action. However, you may still prefer to put all your funds in one personal pension under your own control. You should first discuss these matters with your financial adviser.

If you add up your existing pension rights you can establish your current pension provision. To find out whether that will be enough to keep you in the lifestyle of your choice, you need to estimate how much you will be earning at retirement. If there is a shortfall you will need to make some extra investments.

Golden twenties

The current pensions climate with its focus on personal pensions is especially favourable for people in their twenties. Many people within fifteen to twenty years of retirement are really envious of the pension opportunities now available for young people. In the past, pension planning was very haphazard and individual choice was hampered due to restrictive and out-dated laws. The great thing about being in your twenties now is that you have the choice of joining the company pension scheme or buying your own personal pension – so, what should you do?

If you expect to stay with your employers for the whole of your working life and if your employers have a good final salary pension scheme, preferably one based on 1/60th (see Chapter Three), then you should seriously consider joining the company scheme. This will ensure that your pension will keep in step with your earnings. If you can put in forty years, you should be sure of an inflation-proofed pension of two-thirds final salary, which means that you should have sufficient income to live on happily once you have retired. However, not many people in their twenties can be sure that they will stay with the same employer for that length of time. Career civil servants, teachers, National Health Service and local authority employees are more fortunate in this respect because they can usually change jobs in the public sector without damaging their pension rights.

Employees in the private sector are more likely to

change jobs from time to time to further their careers, they may move to a new area or even be made redundant. They are therefore more likely to benefit from a personal pension that they can contribute to regardless of which company they are working for or whether they become self-employed. Early leavers, that is people who change jobs before retirement, usually find their pension rights suffer badly. They can, of course, transfer the pension rights from previous employers if they were in those schemes for at least two years, but a totally portable personal pension may well serve them better.

Some employers are willing to contribute to your personal pension if you decide not to join the company pension scheme, however by no means all will adopt this generous attitude. Having a personal pension does not stop you from joining a company scheme, although you cannot then also make contributions into your personal pension plan based on earnings from the company. Later on you may join a company, become a director or a high flyer and be offered accelerated pension rights, in which case you can put your personal pension on ice until you want to retire. Of course, with a personal pension, you also have the right to draw your pension at any age from fifty as you are not bound by company rules which traditionally have fixed retirement ages of sixty for women and sixty-five for men.

As a general rule, people in their twenties should keep their options open and a popular way of doing this is to plump for a personal pension. Around 25% of people aged twenty-five have already taken out personal pension plans. The flexibility offered by this type of plan should particularly appeal to women who are planning career breaks and perhaps a period of part-time work after starting a family.

— How much should you contribute?

This is a very difficult question to answer for people in their twenties. A minimum of 5% of your normal earnings would seem to be rock bottom, to be increased to a higher percentage as your earnings improve. You should expect to pay at least 10%. However, it is best to pay the maximum that the Inland Revenue allows, which is 17.5% of your normal earnings on top of your SERPS rebate. This figure is probably more essential for young women because they can expect to have career breaks to bring up their children. The message underlying all this is, the earlier you start, the better, as your money has more time in which it may grow. You can always reduce your payments later if you think you will have more pension than you need. The cost of delay is amply illustrated in the Additional Voluntary Contributions projections in Table B (page 29).

Example:
Paul Worboys pays £50 a month into his unit-linked AVC from the age of twenty-three until he is sixty and builds up a fund of £110,000. Paul will receive £9,000 more than his brother Terry, because Terry did not start contributing until he was twenty-four, a year older, and therefore will receive a fund of only £101,000. This example uses a fairly pessimistic projection, assuming a growth rate of 8.5%. A more optimistic projection, assuming a growth rate of 13%, shows that Paul at sixty should have a fund £37,000 larger – £322,000 compared with Terry's £285,000.

— Checklist for twenties
● If you are in a company pension scheme read the scheme handbook carefully, then check the last annual statement you received to find out what level of pension you can expect. Don't forget that the employer must contribute to the company scheme

- If it is a final salary scheme based on 60ths, your pension should be good if you stay so you do not need to worry for the time being. However, keep an open mind in case your circumstances change
- If it is a final salary scheme based on 80ths, it will be virtually impossible for you to clock up enough years to get a full two-thirds pension. You should consult your financial adviser about additional voluntary contributions or making alternative investments
- If the scheme is a money purchase scheme check that the combined contributions of you and your employer are at least 15%. If less, consider making additional voluntary contributions (AVCs)
- If you have a personal pension, have you contracted-out of SERPS using your 8.46% National Insurance rebate and incentive? If so, consider adding regular contributions of your own. You can add up to 17.5% of your normal earnings. Money invested now will substantially reduce the level you need to contribute in the long term. Dreams of retiring at fifty may be realised if you invest enough in your pension fund now. If you are not contributing your SERPS rebate to your personal pension, you could ask your pension provider for details about how to contract-out. Provided you give notice before 1 April 1992, you can claim a 2% bonus for one year on top of the 5.8% National Insurance rebate
- If you are planning a career in the fast lane and expect to pay higher rate tax and don't have onerous family commitments, one of the best investments now is a personal pension. Based on current higher tax rates (1991–92) your choice is between receiving £60 net earnings or investing £100 gross into your pension fund up to the statutory limits
- If you do not have any pension arrangements, perhaps because you are currently short of money, then you

could start a personal pension with a National Insurance rebate without having to face any extra outlay. You are effectively trading in SERPS in favour of a privatised scheme which could be better value in the long term. You must remember, however, that you should not rely on a rebate-only pension to give you an adequate retirement income but simply a better return than if you relied on the state

- If, understandably, you don't like the idea of tying up your money until you retire or are in your fifties, you could consider other types of investment. It is better to have some savings earmarked for retirement rather than not to set aside anything at all. Later on you may be able to transfer some of this money into a pension plan if you wish

- If you are self-employed you ought to be aware that you cannot rely on the SERPS pension to top up your basic state pension. By buying a personal pension you can save tax. If you are a basic rate tax-payer, for every £100 you contribute to a personal pension you can knock £25 of your pension contributions off your tax bill, provided that your pension contribution does not exceed 17.5% of your net relevant earnings.

Silver thirties

If you are in your thirties it is fairly likely that you will be married with children and a mortgage and that pension planning might not seem a priority as you struggle to make ends meet! However, you probably have a lifestyle you would be reluctant to give up and are concentrating on your career. Your pension planning may be on the back burner while your earnings are used to finance daily family commitments. It is still worth checking your pension position, because if you delay, you will find higher contributions are needed to generate the level of pension you require. Delay could cost you dearly in your forties and could ruin any hopes of retiring in your fifties.

— *Checklist for thirties*

● If you are in a company pension scheme, read the handbook carefully. Compare it with the last annual statement you received to find out what you could expect if you remain with them

● If you are in a final salary company pension scheme based on 60ths, check whether you can put in a full forty years' service with them. If you can, you should be on course for a good pension and need not worry for the time being

● If you are in a final salary scheme and cannot put in a full forty years – for example, if you have just joined and are thirty-five now, you are likely to be looking at a pension equal to half your current pay. You should consider the virtues of starting AVC contributions now rather than leaving it to later

● If you are in a final salary scheme based on 80ths, then the maximum pension you could expect if you were in the scheme from ages eighteen to sixty-five (or sixty) would be just over half your final pay. If you are aged thirty-five now, the maximum pension you could qualify for would be about 37% of final salary, that is 30/80ths. This means that if you wish to achieve a two-thirds pension you ought to consider contributing to AVCs straightaway. It will be less painful now than in a few years' time (see Table D, page 60)

● If you are in a money purchase company pension scheme, check how much your fund is currently worth. As a rough indicator, if it is in the order of one-quarter of what you think you will need (see Table A, page 17) then you need not worry now

● If you have only recently joined the money purchase scheme you should consider making AVCs. The

27

maximum you are allowed to contribute personally is 15% of your normal salary, regardless of age. There is theoretically no limit to how much your employer can contribute. Therefore, as employees in personal pension plans are allowed to contribute 17.5%, you should aim for a joint contribution (yours added to your employer's) of at least 17.5% up to age thirty-five and 20% from age thirty-six to forty. If that will not be enough to give you a decent pension then you could consider alternative investments

- If you have been in the final salary schemes of previous employers, for at least two years at a time (five years before 1988), then now is the time to consider putting the funds accumulated into your own personal pension or buy-out plan. You should take advice from your personal financial adviser on the best ways to do this, what costs you may incur and the best schemes on the market to suit your requirements

- If you have a personal pension and you are under thirty-six, are you putting in your maximum 17.5% of normal earnings (or net relevant earnings if you are self-employed)? If you are thirty-six or more, are you contributing your maximum 20%? The more money you invest now, the greater the chance that you will be in the position of being able to retire early

- If your current earnings are high, you could consider contributing extra to your personal pension by taking advantage of previous years' unused relief. You can go back six years and claim tax relief at your highest rate paid in the year the contribution is made. At the same time, you can have a contribution treated as though it had been paid in the tax year before it actually was, so in effect you can claim up to seven years' worth of unused relief in one year, as long as your contribution is not larger than your net relevant earnings in that one year. This will give a tremendous boost to your pension fund and may enable you to choose between retiring early, having a better pension or not having to worry about pension contributions later on

- If you are not in a pension scheme at all you should really think seriously about the financial implications of living on a basic state pension, currently £52 a week, plus any other savings you have. Time is beginning to run out before pension planning gets expensive

The following table shows how much a man of thirty-five, planning to invest £100 a month in a pension (or AVC – topping-up pension), could lose by the time he retires at sixty-five if he delays:

Table B: COST OF DELAY

Starts investing	Loss assuming growth at		Capital at retirement assuming growth at	
	8.5% p.a.	13% p.a.	8.5% p.a.	13% p.a.
Now	No loss	No loss	£127,000	£293,000
in 1 year	£10,000	£ 43,000	£117,000	£259,000
in 5 years	£45,000	£136,000	£ 81,500	£157,000
in 10 years	£76,400	£209,800	£ 50,600	£ 83,200

Source: Sun Life, 1991

Fortunate forties
As far as pension planning is concerned, the forties are a crucial period. You still have time to top up without too much pain, although this may mean reducing your take-home pay. By now you should be less worried about the financial commitments of bringing up a family and more

able to concentrate on your own long-term future. If you want to retire on anything like two-thirds final salary, your pension plans should be well under control. If they are not, then you need a plan to make up the shortfall.

— Checklist for forties

- If you are in a final salary scheme based on 60ths and you expect to be able to put in forty years before you retire, then you have nothing to worry about, because you should get two-thirds final salary without any problem
- If you cannot put in forty years, or if you are in a scheme based on 80ths, you cannot achieve two-thirds without topping up your pension plans. You could consider AVCs. Example B in Table A (page 17) will explain how to use AVCs to put your pension back on course
- Directors, executives or key workers may be able to put their pension in the fast lane. If your firm will agree to put you on to an accelerated rate of pension, then you can effectively make up for lost time. In this way you could be qualifying for your pension at the rate of, say, 2/60ths a year. This means that for every year you work for the firm, you get a pension of 2/60ths of a year's pay (see Chapter Six)
- Alternatively, it may be possible for you to arrange to increase your contributions to buy 'added years'. Not all company pension schemes will allow this, but if yours does it is a convenient way of increasing your pension. Check with your scheme manager
- If you are in a company money purchase pension scheme or a personal pension, your fund should now be worth roughly half of what you are aiming for in retirement. That means that if two-thirds of your current pay is £10,000, then your fund ought to be somewhere in the region of £50,000. This is calculated

on the basis that you will be able to get a 10% annuity (see page 69) which will give you a pension of £5,000
- If you are in a company money purchase scheme and your fund does not seem to match your expected requirements, then you ought to consider increasing your own contributions. The legal maximum is 15% of your normal earnings. Although not all companies will allow you to vary your contributions, it is worth asking
- If you are contributing the maximum the law or the company scheme rules allow and you still have a shortfall, then you could consider building up a reserve fund through other investments
- If you have a personal pension, you can contribute 20% of your normal earnings up to your mid-forties and 25% between the ages of forty-six to fifty. Should you start a personal pension? This really depends on whether the company's contribution added to your own exceeds 20% (or 25%). If it does not it might be a good idea to go it alone. Do remember, however, that companies often offer life cover including spouse's pension and lump sum if you die prematurely, as part of their pension package. You should consider very carefully the advantages of staying put, because you may lose these valuable benefits if you die before retirement
- If you are self-employed, without significant alternative resources, it is vital to consider investing in a personal pension. You may hope to sell your business and retire on the money you make, but this is not something you can rely on. It might be worth reconsidering your strategy and having a personal pension as a safety cushion
- It could be worth starting up a personal pension and contributing extra to make up for some of the years when you have missed contributions. You can claim

31

tax relief on contributions made this year and for up to seven years back dated (see Chapter Four). This facility is not confined to the self-employed; employees with personal pensions can do the same

Thrifty fifties
People in their fifties are more likely to have been thrifty throughout their working lives as they were brought up during the era of post-war austerity. While many were denied opportunities to join pension schemes when they were young, they are more likely to have a nest-egg underpinning their retirement planning. Also, some 10% will have had the added bonus of inheriting property from their parents.

People in their fifties can still give their pensions a boost, but it is relatively costly to do so.

— Checklist for fifties
● If you have been fortunate enough to be in a good 1/60th final salary company pension scheme for most of your working life, you could be well on course to an independent retirement. If this is the case then you might be more concerned about getting the best out of other investments
● If you have not been in the company final salary scheme for long enough, you will need to think about topping up your pension. You should consider AVCs if you are not already contributing the full 15% of your normal earnings into your company pension
● If you are an executive or key worker in a firm with a final salary scheme, you could try to negotiate a better deal so that, instead of qualifying for 1/60th per year of service, the company counts each year for the scheme's purpose as if you had been contributing for two years. Your future benefits would be doubled. If you have

fifteen years to go before retirement, that will give you a half-pension (30/60ths)

- If you are in a money purchase company scheme which is not building up fast enough, you could ask to increase your contributions up to the 15% limit of your earnings if you are not already doing this and if the scheme allows you to. The company may be prepared to offer you the facility of a salary sacrifice. This means they drop your pay by an agreed sum and then add it to their contribution to your pension fund, thereby boosting your fund

- Alternatively, if you are fully subscribing or if you would rather build up a lump sum, you could consider alternative investments. You should consult your financial adviser about this

- If your money purchase fund is really lagging behind your requirements, you could consider withdrawing from your company money purchase scheme. This means you leave the contributions invested in the scheme and start up a personal pension where the contribution limits are higher. If your joint contributions – your employer's and your own – don't exceed the personal pension contribution limits and your employer is willing to contribute, it might be a sensible course of action

- If you have a personal pension and the fund needs a boost you may be able to increase your contributions. People aged forty-six to fifty are allowed to contribute 25% of their normal earnings. However, when you are fifty-one to fifty-five, you can contribute 30%, from age fifty-six to sixty you can contribute 35% and at sixty-one plus you can invest 40%. This facility is ideal for late starters and those who need to give their retirement planning a tonic

- If you have had a number of previous jobs, leaving some pension rights behind, it could be a good time to

round them up through a personal pension or buy-out plan arrangement. You should take advice on whether this option is right for you, but it is certainly worth investigating
- If you have no pension plan at all and no private resources to subsidise your retirement income, then you need to act quickly. It is certainly not too late, but you have not left yourself much time. If you start a personal pension then from age forty-six to fifty you can contribute 25% of your normal earnings, from fifty-one to fifty-five you can contribute 30%, from fifty-six to sixty 35% and from sixty-one to seventy-five 40%. You can also take advantage of the seven-year 'carry back, carry forward' facility, assuming you have enough cash to invest
- If you have taken all the necessary action, absorbed all your allowances and still wish to top up your retirement fund efficiently, you could look at alternative investments

CHAPTER TWO:
BREAD AND BUTTER
PENSIONS

For the whole of your working life you will probably have been paying National Insurance contributions and perhaps wondering whether it was all worth it. However, when you reach the statutory pensionable age (sixty for women and sixty-five for men), you will begin to benefit. At this stage you stop paying National Insurance contributions and can at last start getting your money back through the state pension scheme, provided that you have made sufficient contributions. The state actually provides three types of pensions and when planning your retirement finances it is important to understand what you can expect from each of them. The two main pensions are:

● Basic state pension
● Additional state pension – State Earnings Related Pension Scheme (SERPS)

On top of that, people who were working between 1961 and 1975 may qualify for a graduated pension, which was replaced by SERPS, but at best this is only worth about £5 a week.

Basic state pension

The basic state pension is paid to people who have made enough National Insurance contributions throughout their working lives.

The basic state pension is not sufficient to retire on unless you are prepared to live exceedingly economically. Currently (1991–92) the full basic state pension is £52 a week, which amounts to £2,704 per year. The buying power of the state pension is reviewed annually and increased. Nevertheless it tends to make up in consistency what it lacks in value. You can assume that the basic state pension will continue to represent something like 20% of the average national earnings for a single person and 33% for married couples. In times of rising prices that degree of inflation-proofing is a plus that is worth having, even if the pension is increased annually in arrears.

To qualify for the full basic pension you have to pay weekly National Insurance contributions. If you are employed, your employer deducts your payments from your earnings, adds the employer's contribution and pays it to the Department of Social Security. If you are self-employed you have to buy a flat rate Class 2 stamp each week from the Post Office. At present the flat rate stamp costs £5.15 (1991–92). In order to obtain a full state pension you normally need to have paid full National Insurance contributions every week for at least 90% of your working life.

At present (1991–92) there are four classes of National Insurance contribution:

● Class 1
  Paid by all employees earning more than £52 a week and their employers, though some married women who opted to pay a reduced rate can continue to do so. The amount the employees pay varies according to the

level of their earnings up to £390 a week, above which an employee currently pays no more
- Class 2
  Paid by all self-employed people earning more than £2,900 a year at a flat rate of £5.15 a week
- Class 3
  Voluntary contributions, currently £5.05 a week, which you can pay to protect your National Insurance record if you have some missing years
- Class 4
  An additional levy paid by self-employed people, on top of their flat rate contribution, on earnings between £5,900 and £20,280 p.a. Half of the contributions are tax-deductible

A working life is usually defined by the government as forty-four years for women and forty-nine years for men. This means that women need to have paid the full National Insurance contributions for about thirty-nine years and men for about forty-four years. Under normal circumstances, if you have failed to pay full contributions for at least ten years of your working life, you are not entitled to any state pension. There are exceptions to this ten-year rule for special cases such as anyone who takes a career break to bring up children, those who have looked after sick people, those unlucky enough to have been out of work through redundancy, illness or disability and those who were working before 1948 when the pension scheme was introduced.

Not everyone has to pay National Insurance. You only pay it if you earn above a certain sum. If you have not earned enough to pay contributions for the whole of your working life, perhaps because you have been working part-time, your pension will normally be reduced. In the current tax year (1991–92) anyone under state pension-

...ng £52 a week or more has to pay National
...ntributions.

women

...ngs of married women and widows who opted to
pa... the reduced rate, the so-called 'married women's
stamp', do not qualify towards the total of years contributing. This option was withdrawn for newcomers in
April 1977. Also, wives who never paid National Insurance contributions at all cannot qualify for a state
pension in their own right. However, if your husband
qualifies for a state pension, then you qualify for a
married woman's additional pension based on the level
of his contributions. This extra pension is now paid to the
wife once the husband reaches the statutory retirement
age.

At current rates, married women who opted to pay the
reduced stamp and women who have never paid National
Insurance contributions can qualify for a pension of up to
£31.25 per week (£1,625 p.a.) bringing the total for the
couple to £83.25 (£4,329 p.a.). However, on the death of
the husband, the wife receives a widow's pension of £52
per week (£2,704 p.a.) which is the same as a basic
pension.

Career breaks

Special arrangements were introduced in April 1978 for
anyone who stops working for a few years to bring up
their children, providing they are getting child benefit for
children under sixteen. Similar concessions apply to
those people who have given up their job to look after a
sick person and who qualify for income support. Their
basic state pension rights are protected under the Home
Responsibility Protection scheme (HRP). For every year
they are out of work for these reasons they are automatically credited with one qualifying year for their pension.

Married women and widows who have kept up their option to pay the reduced stamp cannot get credits under this scheme.

If you have to stop work to look after someone who is getting an attendance allowance, you should apply for HRP for those years. You must apply annually using Form CF411 which is available from your local Department of Social Security office. Other people who can arrange to protect their pensions include those who have been receiving unemployment benefit, sickness benefit, invalidity benefit or approved training.

Divorce

A divorced woman can use her ex-husband's National Insurance record to protect her pension credits for the period that they were married. Therefore, a woman who either did not pay National Insurance contributions perhaps because she did not work, or earn enough to pay, or elected to pay the married women's stamp, need not lose out, provided her ex-husband paid the full contributions. If his contribution record is insufficient for full credits, then her credits will be scaled down accordingly. If the ex-husband remarries, his new wife will still (subject to his contribution record) qualify for the usual married woman's pension and widow's pension. The husband is treated as though he had only been married once.

The self-employed

The self-employed qualify for the basic state pension through their Class 2 flat rate contribution. If they also have to pay Class 4 National Insurance contributions based on their profits, this will make no difference to their pension. A self-employed year is treated the same as an employed year. So, if you have worked for an employer in the past, those years are added to your self-employed years, provided you have kept up your regular contributions.

SERPS
SERPS is the state's additional earnings related pension scheme for employees and company directors. It is paid on top of the basic state pension out of the earnings-related National Insurance contributions.

It is possible to contract-out of SERPS, in which case you will not qualify for the state top-up scheme for the period that you are contracted-out. Sometimes company pension schemes have opted out in favour of getting a National Insurance rebate which they invest in their pension fund for employees, and the employees have no option. However, if it is a final salary scheme the company has to guarantee that you will not lose by the deal (see Chapter Three for further details).

The benefits of SERPS are based solely on your earnings between the so-called Lower Earnings Level (£52 per week in 1991–92) and the Upper Earnings Level (£390 per week in 1991–92). The maximum anyone who retires in 1991, has been in SERPS since it started and paid the top level of contributions during that period, can expect is the far from princely sum of £2,400 p.a. (1991–92). Since the government has announced plans to reduce SERPS payments, the value of this earnings-related portion will decline further in the future.

— Spouses
If a widow inherits a SERPS pension from her late husband, she will be paid the same sum he would have received provided that he reaches state retirement age of sixty-five before 5 April 2000. If he dies after that she will only get 50% because the scheme starts to reduce after 1999.

A widower can only inherit his late wife's SERPS

pension if she had reached state retirement age before dying and if he had retired from regular employment. It can then be used to top up his pension to the maximum SERPS any individual could qualify for. That means that if he was already getting the maximum SERPS pension he would not get any more.

The self-employed do not qualify for SERPS but they retain any SERPS credits they qualified for if they have worked for an employer at some time during their working life after 6 April 1978, when SERPS was introduced.

— Graduated Pensions
Before SERPS was introduced there was a state pension scheme called Graduated Pensions, which related to earnings. It ran from 1961 to 1975 and was not very generous. However, people who have paid into it through their old National Insurance contributions can expect to get something from it. The maximum you can expect is about £5.50 a week for men and £4.50 for women if you were very well paid during that period, but most people can expect significantly less than inflation.

Getting a state pension forecast
You can find out at any time what state pensions you are likely to get and what, if anything, you can do about improving them. All you have to do is to get Form BR19, 'How you can get a Retirement Pension Forecast', from your local office of the Department of Social Security (their address will be in the local phone book). You fill it in and send it back to their office in Newcastle-upon-Tyne, and about a month later you should get the answers.

This pensions forecast is a most useful start to pension planning, and it has been well thought out so that you can ask questions – "what if . . . ?"

Basically, the forecast will tell you:

- How much pension you are already entitled to (basic state pension, SERPS and Graduated Pension), based on your contributions so far
- How much pension you will be entitled to at sixty (for women) and sixty-five (for men), if you pay National Insurance contributions until then
- What, if anything, you can do to get a better state pension
- If you are widowed or divorced, the amount of pension you can expect from the three state schemes, based on your former spouse's National Insurance contributions

The forecast will also tell you what may happen to your state pensions in different situations. For example, you can ask how much your pensions will be if:

- You intend to carry on working past retirement age. You will need to give them a possible date
- You want to retire early. You will need to give them a possible date. You won't be able to claim your pension early and it will probably be reduced
- You want to go abroad
- You want to start paying full rate National Insurance contributions after having paid reduced rate
- You want to pay National Insurance contributions that have not been paid in the past
- Change of marital status. You will need to give them a possible date for getting married or divorced
- Change in annual earnings. If you expect a significant rise and are not in a contracted-out pension scheme this might affect your SERPS pension. Alternatively, you might be expecting a drop in earnings

So, as you can see, the Department of Social Security have tried to be realistic in their approach to helping you to plan your retirement income. In Appendix One we look at the type of information they can supply you with concerning your state pension rights.

We asked the Department of Social Security to give us two quotations: one for a man and one for a woman both aged fifty and earning £15,000. They have been earning at a similar level in the past, so earnings in earlier years have been adjusted for inflation. They have both put in ten years of SERPS, but have both been in contracted-out schemes for the past three years.

During the past thirteen years the woman has had a career break of three years to bring up her one child, hence she qualifies for Home Responsibility Protection for three years. However, as she had earlier opted to pay the married woman's reduced National Insurance contributions for a while, effectively she has only been qualifying for state pensions for thirteen years, since April 1978. But she can use her husband's National Insurance contributions to increase her potential basic pension to 60%.

The results show that at April 1991:

	Mr A	Mrs A
Total state pensions already qualified for	£64.22	£41.03

(If they were allowed to retire tomorrow this is what they would get)

	Mr A	Mrs A
Total pensions at normal retirement age if they continue paying National Insurance	£77.61	£59.29

This breaks down into three categories, basic pension, SERPS and Graduated Pension, as follows:

Basic pension

Already qualified for   £40.56 (78%)   £19.24 (37%)

Payable at retirement if
they continue to pay
National Insurance   £52.00 (100%)   £33.28 (64%)

Notes:
- Mr A cannot improve his basic pension by any increased National Insurance contributions because he is up to date
- Mrs A cannot improve her basic pension because she cannot pay voluntary contributions for missing years if they are for a period more than six years earlier

Serps – 'Additional pension'

	Mr A	Mrs A
Situation now:		
Without contracting-out	£26.77	£26.02
Less contracted-out deduction (three years)	£ 5.15	£ 6.27
Total payable now	£21.62	£19.75
At retirement:		
Without contracting-out	£54.70	£51.32
Less contracting-out deduction (three years)	£31.13	£27.35
Total payable	£23.57	£23.97

Graduated Pension
(thirty units)   £ 2.04   £ 2.04

Extra information given:

Mr A: A man can get automatic credits instead of having to pay National Insurance contributions for the five full tax years starting with the one in which he is sixty, if he is not working, or if he is working but not earning enough to qualify for paying National Insurance. He won't qualify, however, if he spends more than 182 days abroad in any one tax year.

Mrs A: If Mrs A stops working when she is fifty-five (7 July 1996), then her pension, at retirement age, would be £49.84.

When can you draw your state pensions?

The state pensions are payable when you reach the current statutory retirement age, sixty for women and sixty-five for men, whether you have retired or not. You have to draw them all at once – you cannot draw them one at a time.

However, there are special restrictions about a woman drawing the married woman's additional pension, which is only payable by virtue of her husband's contributions. (This may also apply in reverse where the woman's contributions qualify her husband for the additional pension.) A woman cannot receive a married woman's pension, currently £31.25 a week (£1,625 p.a.), until her husband reaches sixty-five. If a woman is under sixty when her husband retires at sixty-five her pension will be paid direct to him. She will have to wait until she is sixty to receive it herself. If her own pension equals or exceeds the standard rate of the additional pension, currently £31.25 per week (£1,625 p.a.), then she will not be entitled to draw the additional pension. She can only draw a sum that brings her own reduced pension up to the level of the additional pension.

— *Early retirement*
If you retire early you cannot claim your state pensions at that stage; you will have to wait until the statutory retirement age. However, even if you are not earning any money, you may well need to make Class Three contributions to protect your basic pension if you have not got enough years' credits – thirty-nine for women and forty-four for men. These contributions are made on a voluntary basis and at a flat rate of £5.05 per week (1991–92).

— *Late retirement*
If you are employed and you wish to retire after the statutory retirement age, you do not have to pay any more National Insurance contributions (although your employer has to continue paying his contributions in the usual way). If you are self-employed you do not have to pay any more Class 2 contributions either but you have to pay Class 4 ones based on your profits for one more year. In either case you can choose whether to draw your state pension immediately you qualify for it or to delay drawing it until such time as you wish. By delaying drawing your state pension you can increase its subsequent value.

Your top-up options
You can increase your state pensions by delaying drawing them for anything up to five years beyond the statutory retirement age. Your pensions will increase by about 7.5% each year and this will be inflation-proofed.

This means that at the end of five years your pension will have grown by about 37.5% over and above the rate of inflation. The decision you make on when to retire will affect all your state pensions. You cannot draw one and delay the rest.

Example:
Deferring your state pensions at today's figures (1991–92)

	Weekly Pension this year	Increments earned after 1 year	after 5 years
Basic Pension	£52.00	£3.85	£19.31
SERPS	£11.70	£0.86	£ 4.35
Graduated Pension	£ 4.00	£0.30	£ 1.48
	£67.70	£5.01	£25.14

Therefore, after one year, the pension increases to £72.71 and after five years it increases to £92.84 at today's figures, but it will be inflation-proofed. You need to consider whether this is worthwhile. If you defer your pension for five years, how long does it take to make up what you have given up? It works out that you start getting your money back in 13.3 years. The calculation below shows how to work this out, assuming current prices throughout because the inflation-proofing element will maintain the buying power of your pension.

(a)	basic pension given up this year	£ 2,704
(b)	multiply by 5 (years)	× 5
(c)	total pension given up	£13,520

To find your pension from year 6
(d)	pension now	£ 2,704
add		
(e)	(d) multiplied by 37.5%	£ 1,014

(f)   enhanced pension   £ 3,718

To establish the number of years you need to draw the enhanced pension to break even:

(g)   divide (c) $$\frac{£13,520}{£\ 1,014} = 13.33 \text{ years}$$

      by (e)

A man would therefore have to live until he was eighty-three before breaking even and a woman would have to live to seventy-eight. Therefore, if you are not in good health you might be better off drawing the pensions.

If you have already started drawing your pensions you can arrange to stop drawing them in order to take advantage of the increments and you can start drawing your pensions again at any time.

Any woman who is entitled to receive the married woman's pension can defer drawing it until she herself reaches age sixty-five, even if her husband is drawing his basic pension. Similarly, a woman who is widowed before age sixty can defer drawing the widow's pension until she is sixty-five. A woman who is widowed after age sixty gets any basic state pension that her husband was entitled to. In each case the pension will increase by about 7.5% a year to a maximum of 37.5% after five years and be inflation-proofed. The pension can be taken at any time of your choice. If a woman's husband does not draw his state pension, perhaps to save paying tax on it because he is still working, then the married woman's pension must be deferred as well. It too however will benefit from the increments.

Missing years

Some people cannot hope to qualify for a full basic state pension, so they are allowed to buy in any missing years at a reduced rate while keeping up their payments at the full rate if they are still working. These are called voluntary contributions and are paid in 1991–92 at a flat rate of £5.05 a week. These contributions will not qualify towards your SERPS pension. Full details are available in leaflets NI42 'National Insurance Voluntary Contributions', and NI48 'National Insurance Unpaid and Late Contributions'. Both leaflets are available free from your local Department of Social Security office.

Married women and widows who opted to pay the married women's stamp are not allowed to buy back those years. However, it may be worthwhile for them to start paying the full contributions in future provided their earnings are sufficient, that is more than £52 a week. They may then be able to start earning credits to get a pension in their own right. But is it worth it? It all depends on your individual circumstances. In order to qualify for the minimum amount of state pension you need to clock up the equivalent of ten years' worth of contributions at the full rate, including those years before you took up your married women's stamp option. Those ten years will give you a quarter pension, currently £13 a week (£676 p.a.). To break even you will need to pay the full stamp for a total of twenty-four years. It hardly seems likely to be worth it. If you are in this situation you are advised to get individual advice from your local Department of Social Security office.

More top-ups

If you have a dependent child or children for whom you are claiming child benefit when you start drawing a state pension, then you may be able to claim an extra payment of up to £10.70 per week (1991–92) for each child. The government also provides a safety net for pensioners who really can't live on the pension; providing they have only minimal savings, pensioners can apply for income support to increase their income and for housing benefit if they need help to pay the rent and/or community charge. Income support may be paid to people with savings and investments of up to £8,000, but the amount is scaled down once the total exceeds £3,000. Housing benefit may be paid to people with savings and investments, excluding the house they live in, of up to £16,000, though the amount is scaled down once the total exceeds £3,000.

Why the state pension is not enough
Even with all these top-ups, it is clear that few people would be able to exist satisfactorily on state pensions. The most an individual could qualify for if they retired this year (1991) and their earnings had at least equalled Upper Earnings Level since 1978, is £5,104. A married couple, reliant on the husband's National Insurance contributions, could only expect £6,729. This is clearly inadequate for a contented retirement, so it is essential that you take charge of your own pension arrangements and try to secure a more prosperous future.

CHAPTER THREE: UNDERSTANDING COMPANY PENSIONS

Since the state can't afford to pay everyone a good pension, they encourage employers to set up pension schemes for their employees. The state, through the Inland Revenue, offers both employers and employees some tax incentives in order to make pension provision more attractive, and hence some very good pension schemes have been devised. These schemes are based on the deferred pay principle, so that any contributions you and your employer make are effectively part of your pay which are invested on your behalf.

Occupational pension schemes are particularly good if you expect to stay with the company for any length of time, and are probably unbeatable if you will be there for the greater part of your working life. They won't be such good value if you expect to be on the move after a couple of years or so because you won't have enough time to build up your pension rights. You will lose significant amounts of pension if you leave the scheme after a short space of time. If you do expect to change jobs a few times in your working life you should consider taking out a personal pension.

If you are a civil servant or work for local authorities or employers like the National Health Service you don't usually need to worry about the effect on your pension of changing jobs, provided that you remain in the public sector. They run very good adaptable occupational pension schemes, and they can usually transfer your pension rights as you move on so you shouldn't be penalised. Also, if you are a woman, any career breaks you have, to bring up the family for instance, are less likely to interfere too much with your pension rights. You will get a smaller pension than if you had an uninterrupted career, but you will usually be better off than most women in the private sector.

This is how occupational pension schemes work. It is generally accepted that a comfortable income in retirement is two-thirds of your salary at the time of your retirement, so many schemes are devised with the objective of giving you this two-thirds if you stay with the company for long enough. Fortunately, the Inland Revenue has a kindly tax regime on pension planning to help you realise this ambition.

As an employee you have a number of ways of aiming for a two-thirds pension:

● Joining an occupational pension scheme
● Starting a personal pension plan
● Saving more

We will describe the main features of each approach and explain the pros and cons. This will help you decide which is best for you, taking into account your age, likely career profile and investment attitude.

— *Occupational pension schemes*
There are two main types of occupational pension scheme:

● Final salary

52

● Money purchase

There are also hybrid schemes which are a mixture of both.

Final salary

A good final salary scheme is the 'Rolls Royce' of pensions, provided that you have been a member for long enough to reap the full benefit. This type of scheme is favoured by the civil service, many top multinational companies and, incidentally, many pension companies for their own staff.

There are currently more people in final salary schemes (also known as defined benefit schemes) than any other type of occupational pension scheme. The range of benefits varies from scheme to scheme. Typically however, you will contribute some 5% of your pay into the scheme and your employers will contribute something like 10%. Some firms have non-contributory schemes in which only the employer contributes. Either way, the money is invested in a pension fund and regardless of how well the investment managers perform, you are guaranteed a certain level of pension, unless the firm itself collapses or the company decides to terminate the scheme.

The pension you get from final salary schemes is related directly to the amount of your salary when you retire. How much this will be depends on three main factors: your salary when you retire (or leave the scheme), the number of years you are in the scheme and the mathematical formula on which the scheme is based, i.e. 60ths or 80ths. If the scheme calculates pensions in 80ths then, for every year you are in the scheme, you will get a pension of 1/80th of your salary at normal retirement age. Therefore, at its simplest, if your salary at retirement is £20,000, you have been in the scheme for twenty years and the scheme is based on 80ths, your pension will be £5,000.

It is worked out like this:

$$£20,000 \times 20/80\text{ths} = £5,000.$$

If you are in an 80ths scheme and you want to achieve an occupational pension equal to two-thirds of your final salary then you will need to stay with the scheme for about fifty-three years; if you join a 60ths scheme you will need to be in it for forty years. In these days of high job mobility it is unlikely that many people will actually stay long enough with one company to qualify for the two-thirds maximum.

Some companies offer directors and key personnel an 'uplifting' facility, which gives them more than the standard 1/60th or 1/80th pension for each year they contribute. They may, for example, give them 2/60ths or 2/80ths for each year. If employees get 2/60ths for each year then they can qualify for a full two-thirds pension after twenty years. Likewise, if they are allowed 2/80ths they can qualify for a full two-thirds final salary after twenty-seven years. It is not possible now to qualify for a two-thirds pension in less than twenty years, but anyone who was in the pension scheme prior to 17 March 1987 may qualify for this maximum after ten years, subject to the pension scheme rules.

There is another restriction related to the maximum pension anyone can draw from an occupational scheme if they joined it after 1 June 1989, or 14 March 1989 if it was a new scheme. There is now an 'earnings cap', which means that you cannot get a pension based on earnings in excess of £71,400. Taken together with the two-thirds rule, this means the maximum occupational pension is £47,600 in 1991–92. This figure is adjusted annually in line with the Retail Prices Index. Employees who were in the scheme before the new rules applied are only limited by the two-thirds final salary rule.

To complicate matters more, the definition of final salary varies from scheme to scheme. In some schemes it is literally your basic salary on retirement, others include bonuses and overtime and some are based on average salaries in the years prior to retirement. The rules are stricter for directors. In addition, some final salary schemes add the basic state pension when quoting you a two-thirds final salary pension. This means that they are offering to top up your basic state pension to ensure your total pension income equals two-thirds of your final salary – or a proportion of it. Also, if the scheme has been contracted-out of SERPS, part of the pension they quote will include the SERPS element for the period that you worked for them and you will not get that from the state as well. Apart from the public sector pensions, for the civil service and local authorities for instance which are fully inflation-proofed, very few occupational final salary schemes are even partially inflation-proofed.

In 1990 the government introduced legislation to require partial inflation-proofing of pensions in payment. However, it is unclear when this will come into force and whether or not it will apply to benefits accrued in the past.

A good final salary scheme will allow your widow/er to have a pension equal to about two-thirds of your own if you die before they do. It should also include a decent life assurance package. This is a valuable employee benefit because it will pay out a significant lump sum to your widow/er if you die before you retire, as well as leaving them with a reasonable pension of some two-thirds of the pension you would have drawn. There may also be provision for payments to be made if you have to stop work before your normal retirement age because of illness or a serious accident under a separate scheme.

— SERPS
If you join or belong to a contracted-out final salary

pension scheme then you cannot also qualify for a State Earnings Related Pension Scheme pension (SERPS) during the time that you are in the company scheme. SERPS is designed to top up your state pension in relation to your earnings.

Most final salary schemes which contract out do so by providing a certain level of benefit. They do this by guaranteeing that you will get an equivalent sum to your SERPS pension. This is called the Guaranteed Minimum Pension (GMP) and is incorporated in your company pension. The GMP portion of your pension has to be partly inflation-proofed for the whole of your life and must now include a spouse's pension rights to half GMP, similarly inflation-proofed. The level of inflation-proofing is the Retail Prices Index or 3%, whichever is the lower. The state makes up the shortfall.

— *The advantages of a final salary scheme*

A final salary scheme is usually good value if you expect to stay with the firm for most of your working life. A big plus is that the company typically contributes twice as much to it as you do. Once you are in the scheme they are committed to giving you a certain level of pension, regardless of how much they have in the pension fund.

As your pension is related to your final salary you know what you can expect and that your pension will increase in line with your career progress throughout the firm. Therefore, the earlier you join the scheme the better because you will qualify for a bigger pension the longer you are in the scheme. This predictability is a major asset when you are planning your retirement.

If your pension is unlikely to be sufficient, you have time to make alternative plans to top up your retirement income. The following table will help you assess whether you will have enough.

Table C: FINAL SALARY – ANNUAL PENSION
For every £1,000 of your final salary you can expect an annual pension of:

Years in scheme	60th scheme £	80th scheme £
1	16.66	12.50
5	83.30	62.50
10	166.60	125.00
15	250.00	187.50
20	333.33	250.00
25	416.60	312.50
30	500.00	375.00
35	583.30	437.50
40	666.66	500.00

Assumption: that you do not commute any of your pension

From the table you can work out that, if you expect to be in the company's 1/60th scheme for a total of thirty years and are earning £20,000 a year now, you will get a pension of at least £10,000 at today's figures, unless you take a lesser post. If you get promoted, your pension will increase pro rata. If you will be satisfied with £10,000 (at today's figures) plus SERPS, assuming the scheme is not contracted-out, then you have nothing to worry about.

However, if you would like a bigger pension then you can make additional arrangements. The simplest way of doing this is by starting an Additional Voluntary Contribution (AVC) plan or by investing in Personal Equity Plans (PEPs).

— *AVCs*
Every final salary scheme has to allow you the facility to

have an AVC. You can either choose their plan or select one of your own. If you buy AVCs privately they are called Freestanding AVCs (FSAVCs). These are specifically designed for employees in company final salary pension schemes. They work like personal pensions. You build up your own private pension fund so that when you retire you can buy an annuity (an income for life) with the money. You can contribute as much as you like, provided that the total money you are contributing towards your pensions – including your contributions to the company scheme – does not exceed 15% of your normal earnings. That means that if you are already paying 5% to the company scheme you can invest up to 10%. If you are lucky enough to be in a non-contributory pension scheme, then you can invest up to the full 15% in AVCs. Your employer's contributions do not count when calculating your investment ceiling.

Your contributions to the company AVCs are paid out of your earnings before tax is deducted. So if you pay income tax at 25%, and your monthly contribution is £20, your take-home pay will only be reduced by £15.

If, however, you are a basic rate tax payer then FSAVCs are paid out of your net earnings. You pay contributions net and these are credited with tax paid at the basic rate i.e. 25%. Higher rate taxpayers have to reclaim the additional tax relief through their annual tax return.

Whether you buy AVCs through the company scheme or privately depends mainly on a couple of factors:

● Investment performance. A private scheme may offer you a better return because the insurance company you favour has a better track record than the insurance company that runs your firm's scheme. However, if the insurance company you favour is the same as the insurance company your firm uses, you will normally get better terms by investing in the company scheme.

Management charges will cost less because the company benefits from bulk sales
- Independence. You may prefer to be independent and back your own judgement and even take a bit of a gamble by buying unit-linked AVCs rather than those on offer through the company scheme
- Portable. If you think you may leave the firm to join another one before you retire you can take your FSAVC plan with you and continue contributing to it. If you have a company AVC, then you have to leave the money untouched when you go and if you wish to transfer, you will only be able to do so at the same time as you transfer the main scheme benefits. You will be able to convert it into an annuity when you retire

You should not buy AVCs in the unlikely event that you expect to get the full two-thirds final salary pension from your occupational scheme with the maximum other benefits like spouse's and increases in pension, because the Inland Revenue will not allow you to draw a single penny more than two-thirds of final salary. If you want to top up your pension, you ought to consult the company pensions administrator, to see what size the potential shortfall is likely to be.

There are other reasons for buying AVCs, apart from topping up your pension because you cannot put in enough time to build it up to the full two-thirds final salary permissible. It may be sensible to buy them in order to take the maximum tax-free lump sum from the company scheme, while protecting your retirement income. Also, provided you do not risk busting the two-thirds limit, you can buy AVCs to build in what is effectively an element of inflation-proofing to your retirement income. You don't have to convert your AVCs into an annuity when you retire. You can leave your fund to build up for a while and buy your annuity later but you must take the benefits at the same time as you take the company benefits. You are never too young to buy AVCs. You can start buying them as soon as you join the company pension scheme. As it is your own private fund, you can put it on ice if you leave the firm or can continue contributing to it, if it is a FSAVC, when you start your new job.

Young people are now being encouraged to contribute to AVCs while they are 'footloose and fancy-free' and not yet committed to the expense of bringing up a young family. They are beginning to appeal to young high earners who pay tax at the higher rate and are thinking of retiring early. The saying 'it's the early bird who catches the worm' is clearly illustrated in the following table which highlights the cost of delay in contributing to AVCs (or FSAVCs).

Table D: AVC (CONTRACTED-IN) PROJECTIONS
Basis: Male wanting to retire at sixty pays £50 a month into a unit-linked AVC plan

| Age at outset | Assuming rate of growth | | | |
	8.5%		13%	
	Size of fund at age 60	Loss from delaying 1 year	Size of fund at age 60	Loss from delaying 1 year
25	£93,400	£7,000	£252,000	£28,400
30	£60,600	£4,600	£136,000	£15,400
35	£38,500	£2,800	£ 73,200	£ 8,100
40	£23,800	£1,700	£ 38,500	£ 4,100
45	£13,900	£1,000	£ 19,500	£ 2,100
50	£ 7,210	£ 460	£ 8,840	£ 890

Source: Sun Life, 1991

— Personal Equity Plans

Personal Equity Plans (PEPs) can be ideal vehicles for building up a lump sum for retirement as an additional part of your pension planning, either because you cannot put in enough time with your employers to get a full two-thirds pension, or because you will get the maximum pension but would like to improve upon it.

The great merit of PEPs – apart from probably increasing your capital – is that while you don't get any tax relief when you buy them, any capital gains and dividend income are tax-free when you take them.

PEPs are savings plans which invest substantially in United Kingdom stocks and shares. They are widely available from most insurance companies and unit trust companies, though it is possible to buy them direct from some stockbrokers. Most of them have unit trust funds at their core, but the advantage over unit trusts is that any dividends you receive as income, or arrange to be reinvested, are tax-free. If you leave the dividends to accumulate then your fund will grow even faster. However, come retirement day, you can arrange to start receiving the income, or you can start cashing in the PEPs in easy stages in order to pep up your income if your pension is insufficient. They can also be cashed in for a lump sum to cover one-off expenses.

You can buy PEPs with a lump sum or through a monthly savings plan, or both, whichever arrangement suits you best. But you can only open one plan a year. A husband and wife can have a plan each, thereby spreading the investment more widely. Because they are invested in stocks and shares, there is a risk that the value of PEPs will go down, but it is possible to buy less risky PEPs. Your financial adviser should be able to recommend a PEP that suits your investment philosophy. The closer you are to retirement, say four or five years, the less risk you should take. But over the distance good unit trusts have historically given you much better returns than building society high interest deposit accounts.

All adults are currently (1991–92) allowed to invest up to £6,000 a year in ordinary PEPs, which means that a husband and wife can invest up to £12,000 a year between them. As from January 1992 you will be allowed to invest a further £3,000 each, on top of the £6,000, in a new Corporate PEP. These schemes will enable each of you to invest up to £3,000 in a single company in a PEP. Full details are not yet available because they don't come into operation until the New Year, but they are worth watching out for.

— Disadvantages of a final salary pension scheme

The main disadvantage of a final salary scheme is that it usually offers pretty poor value for early leavers or job-hoppers. People change jobs for a number of reasons. In certain types of occupation, such as publishing, advertising, motor sales and the leisure industry, high flyers need to change jobs to improve their career prospects and income. Alternatively they may be in the construction industry and work on contracts. Redundancy also takes its toll in some cyclical industries and means that the employees have little say in their length of service.

— Early leavers

Final salary pension schemes are designed for long-stayers who will remain with the same company until retirement. These schemes are not geared up for mobile workforces and penalise participants when they leave after a couple of years although legislation over the past decade has improved the unhappy lot of the early leaver. If you are in a final salary scheme for less than two years, you are not entitled to anything more than a return of your own contributions, not even the contributions the firm has made on your behalf. This is particularly damaging to people who join a non-contributory pension scheme and leave before two years, because they get nothing back and have lost the opportunity to make any pension provision for themselves! Those who get their money back will receive it in cash less a special rate of tax of 20% and that cannot be claimed back even if they are non-taxpayers.

If the scheme has contracted-out of SERPS there will probably be a hefty deduction which the company will pay to the Department of Social Security to buy back your rights for the state top-up scheme for the time you were employed. You do not usually get any interest on the money you receive, about one-third of companies are believed to pay interest and if they do it is usually at a pretty low rate. So, the overall return on your money is rather dismal.

People who get this return of funds tend to spend it when it would be wiser to invest it in a personal pension. As the Inland Revenue will assume that such people have not been in a company pension scheme for the period that the 'rebate' covers, they are entitled to contribute to a personal pension under the 'carry forward/carry back' rules, which effectively enables them to backdate payments for up to seven years. If you put in more than two years you cannot draw the cash as such, but you don't lose it. You have three main options. You can:

● Accept a deferred pension
● Arrange to transfer your pension rights to your new employer's pension scheme
● Buy a deferred annuity (a buy-out bond) or transfer the money into your own special personal pension

— Deferred pension

The company must offer you the right to a deferred pension which you can draw at retirement age. However, the deferred pension is based on the number of years that you were in the pension scheme, your salary on leaving the firm and whether the scheme was based on 60ths or 80ths. At its simplest this means that if you are earning £15,000 when you leave a final salary scheme at age thirty after six years in the scheme which is based on 80ths and your normal retirement age is sixty, you will be entitled to a pension of £1,125 in thirty years' time (£15,000 × 6/80). If you leave in 1991 or after, any deferred pension rights you qualify for must be partly inflation-proofed, either by the Retail Prices Index or 5%, whichever is the lower. If the scheme is contracted-out, then the position will be more complicated. Your scheme booklet will fill you in with the details. The disadvantage is that a deferred pension does not take into account any future pay increases (which tend to exceed inflation) so it will be based on your earnings at whatever level you had reached in your career at thirty.

Example:

Twins Patrick and Norman who each earn £20,000 are due to retire this year from the same firm. Patrick has had four jobs and has always joined his company's final salary scheme and will get deferred pensions from the first three. Norman has worked with the same firm for forty years, during which time he has been in the final salary pension scheme. All schemes are based on 80ths and are contracted-in. Norman's pension will be nearly £6,000 better than Patrick's. Why?

Table E: COST OF JOB CHANGES

	Number of years in scheme	Leaving salary	Pension	Calculation
Norman	40	£20,000	£10,000	£20,000 × 40/80
Patrick				
Job 1	10	£ 500	£ 62.50	£ 500 × 10/80
Job 2	10	£ 2,000	£ 250.00	£ 2,000 × 10/80
Job 3	10	£10,000	£1,250.00	£10,000 × 10/80
Job 4	10	£20,000	£2,500.00	£20,000 × 10/80
Total pension			£4,062.50	

Note: This assumes the likely fact that none of the schemes offered any element of inflation-proofing prior to 1985. Any deferred pension qualified for after 1985 must now be increased by at least 5% per annum. If you leave in 1991 or later, all the deferred pension must be increased.

In future the position of the early leavers will be better, but by no means as good as the stayers. If we re-cast the figures assuming that the 5% rule had been in place since before Patrick left his first job, we see that his ultimate pension score improves by £1,407 a year to £4,569 which is still £5,431 less than his twin brother!

Table F: PENSION OPTIONS

	Number of years in scheme	Leaving salary	Pension without inflation proofing	Deferred pension increased by 5% p.a.
Norman	40	£20,000	£10,000	–
Patrick				
Job 1	10	£ 500	£ 62.50	£ 270

Job 2	10	£ 2,000	£ 250.00	£ 663
Job 3	10	£10,000	£1,250.00	£2,036
Job 4	10	£20,000	£2,500.00	£2,500
Total pension			£4,062.50	£5,469

Despite this modicum of inflation-proofing, deferred pensions are not very good value for money in the long run. It might be better to transfer your pension rights to your new employer or to your own pension fund. If you left after 1 January 1986, you will be able to transfer any deferred pension rights to your new employers provided they have a suitable scheme and they agree to accept the money. You have no legal rights to transfer your funds if you left before 1986 but, in practice, many pension scheme trustees will allow you to do so.

— Transfer values
The employers you are leaving have to give you a 'transfer value' which should equal the pension rights that you are sacrificing by moving on. Their actuary calculates the transfer value by taking into account your leaving salary, length of service and any benefits you are giving up such as spouse's pension. In basic terms, he works out how much money you would need to invest today to ensure you get the level of benefits on retirement which you have already qualified for. In turn, this transfer value is translated into cash which they pay over to the new employer's pension scheme. In effect, you are using the money to add the past years of service with your previous company to those you will be putting in with your new employer. In practice you will probably lose a year or so in the process unless both employers belong to the same 'transfer club' and have a reciprocal deal which protects the pension.

The other option is to get the money transferred to your

very own pension fund which builds up entirely tax-free until you retire which is when you buy an annuity with it to provide your retirement income. Having worked out your transfer value, your former pension scheme manager pays the money for you into a choice of either a Section 32 buy-out bond which is technically a deferred annuity or personal pension plan.

Buy-out bonds were introduced in 1981 and have special benefits for transfers from contracted-out final salary schemes. They cover the Guaranteed Minimum Pension (GMP) or the SERPS part of your pension, that your employers had opted-out of, as well as investing the rest of the money to enhance your ultimate fund. Pension companies will only accept the transfer if they are sure that the sum is sufficient. You cannot add any new money to a buy-out bond, so if you don't wish to join your new employer's pension scheme and you want to continue contributing to your own pension plan you will have to start a separate personal pension. This is easy enough and nothing to worry about. If anything, it might be more convenient to have two types of your own private pension because this gives you added flexibility.

If, however, you wish to transfer the money to a personal pension then you have various points to consider. If your scheme was contracted-out, the personal pension will not guarantee that the GMP will be paid, but you can take the chance of investing your money to obtain a better benefit. If the personal pension is contracted-out you will have to forego any rights to SERPS, or rights to GMP, for the time you are contributing to it because you will be taking the money from the DSS to pay into your personal pension. You will need to be confident that the pension company investment managers can give you a better return than SERPS, which merely keeps up with inflation. If your personal pension is not contracted-out, i.e. you are not partly funding it with your National Insurance rebate, you will continue to qualify for SERPS. You can transfer your money from the old scheme into a personal pension and at the same time join your new employer's pension scheme. However, if you choose this option, you cannot add any new money to your personal pension plan while you are in the company scheme.

Money purchase pension schemes

Money purchase pension schemes work the same way as personal pensions. The regular contributions you and your employer make are invested in a fund on your behalf and the ultimate size of your pension depends on how well the investments have performed. The contributions are made out of untaxed income. Another tax advantage is that the money in the fund rolls up entirely free of tax, compared with most non-pension savings schemes where any income produced is taxable. They can be contracted-out of SERPS as long as the minimum contribution is made.

When you retire you buy an annuity, which is an income for life, with the funds you have accumulated. As with final salary schemes you will be able to take some of your funds as a lump sum if you wish. If you do so, this will leave less money to generate income unless you reinvest the lump sum.

The disadvantage with money purchase pension schemes is that, unlike final salary schemes, you do not know how much pension you are going to get until you retire. You can make an educated guess when you get close to retirement, but you cannot be absolutely certain. Every year the pension scheme managers must send you a statement telling you how much money your contributions are currently worth and they should give you an idea of what sort of pension that would buy if you continued contributing at the same rate until your normal retirement age. This gives you the opportunity to have an annual pensions audit and check whether your fund is building up at a satisfactory rate.

One advantage of a money purchase scheme is that you usually have scope to increase your contributions if you wish to 'buy' a bigger pension later on. The maximum sum you may contribute annually to a money purchase scheme is 15% of your normal earnings. Anything that your employer contributes does not count against the 15%.

Table G (below) is a guide as to how much pension you can expect from a given lump sum based on various annuity rates. It is a rough guide because, like mortgage interest rates, annuity rates fluctuate. Using a very crude rule of thumb, a woman aged about sixty who wants an annuity which increases by 5% can expect a return of about 8.5%; a man of sixty-five who wants the same type of annuity can expect a return of about 10%; whereas the same man wanting a level income for life regardless of inflation, could possibly get a return of 12.5% on a standard annuity. You should remember that these figures are only a guide. You can only be certain of what pension you will get for your fund when you take your benefits.

Table G: MONEY PURCHASE PENSIONS
Converting money purchase funds into pension income.
How big a fund will you need?

To achieve an annual income of:	Annuity rates		
	8.5%	10%	12.5%
£ 5,000	£ 58,000	£ 50,000	£ 40,000
£10,000	£117,600	£100,000	£ 80,000
£15,000	£176,400	£150,000	£120,000
£20,000	£234,000	£200,000	£160,000

Another important advantage of money purchase schemes is that if you leave the firm before you retire, i.e. you become an early leaver, you may not lose out as badly as you do with a final salary scheme. You have the choice of leaving the money in the fund until you retire, in which case it will keep on growing or you can transfer it to your new employer's scheme (if they agree to accept it). In either case your money will go on working for you. What you cannot do is take the cash and run.

It is easy for the employer you are leaving to work out how much you are owed because it is your fund (or share of the total fund). This can be paid direct into your new scheme, probably with a modest deduction for charges and expenses.

Group personal pensions

Some small firms are now offering their employees the opportunity to invest in group personal pensions which are similar to personal pensions. They are totally portable and you can take them with you if you leave early. The advantage of belonging to them, as opposed to contributing to your own personal pension, is that it is usually cheaper because the company gets a discount off the charges because more than one person, typically a minimum of five employees, is involved. Also, the company is often prepared to contribute to it on your behalf – pound for pound or better – so your fund builds up faster.

Hybrid pension schemes

Some employers offer a scheme which involves elements of both a final salary and a money purchase scheme. The idea is to offer a pension that bears some relation to earnings and which does not penalise the early leaver too badly. In a hybrid scheme the contributions of both employee and employer are shared between two funds.

One fund is a money purchase fund and the other fund is insured and builds up separately. The two together guarantee the employer a salary-related pension based on, say, 100ths so that for every year the employee is in the scheme he is guaranteed a pension of 100th of his final salary.

How much does joining the company pension scheme cost you?

Your contributions are eligible for tax relief, which means that for every £1 you contribute as a basic rate taxpayer, your take-home pay is only reduced by 75p. If the scheme is contracted-out of SERPS you will pay reduced National Insurance contributions, if you currently pay the full rate. Your basic state pension will not be affected, but your SERPS pension will be absorbed into the company scheme.

Table H: COST OF JOINING A COMPANY PENSION SCHEME

(A) Pensionable salary	(B) Contributions as % of salary			(C) Contributions after tax relief			(D) NI contribution reduction	(E) Real cost (C) minus (D)		
	3%	4%	5%	3%	4%	5%		3%	4%	5%
	i	ii	iii	i	ii	iii		i	ii	iii
£	£	£	£	£	£	£	£	£	£	£
3,000	90	120	150	68	90	113	60	8	30	53
8,000	240	320	400	180	240	300	160	20	80	140
13,000	390	520	650	293	390	488	260	33	130	228
16,000	480	640	800	360	480	600	316	44	160	284

Assumptions:
● Income tax payable at 25%

71

- Pensionable salary is annual earnings less £2,704
- The reduction in National Insurance contributions is 2% of pensionable salary

Source: Sun Life, 1991

How to read the table:
If your pensionable pay in column (A) is £16,000 p.a. and you are contributing 5% of your salary to the scheme, this will amount to £600 after tax relief shown in column (C) (iii).

If your employer's scheme is contracted-in, then the 2% National Insurance reduction won't apply.

What happens when you retire?
Four months before you retire, the Department of Social Security should automatically write and tell you how much state pension you can expect. However, at least six months before you retire you should ask your employers, and your AVC supplier if you have bought AVCs independently, how much pension you should get from them.

Different rules apply depending on whether you are in a final salary scheme or a money purchase scheme.

If you are in a final salary scheme you should ask:

- What is the maximum pension you have qualified for
- What is the maximum lump sum you could get if you commute the pension, and what size pension will that leave you with

(For a comparison, you could also ask what pension you would get if you only took half the available lump sum)

If you are married:

● What will your spouse's pension be if you die before they do? Typically it will be two-thirds of your own pension

If there is no automatic provision for a spouse's pension:

● Do you have the option of accepting a reduced pension for yourself in favour of arranging for a spouse's pension? If so, ask for the figures, both before and after commutation

If you are in a money purchase scheme, your fund will be used to buy you an annuity, so you should ask:

● How much money is in your fund
● What is the maximum lump sum you can expect if you commute part of it
● What size annuity you can expect
  a) If you don't commute it
  b) If you commute it
● Can you transfer your money and buy an annuity from the company of your own choice? If so, will they penalise you, and if so, by how much

Armed with all this information you should be in a position to make some decisions, but in Chapter Seven, we go into detail as to whether or not to commute your pension. We also explain the various types of annuities available to employees in money purchase schemes, whether company schemes or personal pensions.

What happens when you die?
If you die before your normal retirement age without

having started to draw your occupational pension, your dependants may be entitled to a lump sum payment of anything up to four times your salary at death, regardless of how many years you have been in the pension scheme. They may get a refund of all your contributions with or without interest and a pension equal to two-thirds of your pension (i.e. 4/9ths of your salary) as well. Further, if you have any children under sixteen, they may be entitled to a pension until they are sixteen.

This money doesn't necessarily come out of the employer's pension fund. It is more likely to come from an insurance company, if the firm has suitable insurance, and therefore employees in money purchase schemes may also qualify for this arrangement. But you will need to check with your employers – just because you are in a pension scheme does not mean that full 'death in service' benefits are available.

If they are available, the trustees of the pension scheme have the discretion to decide the destination of the money. But it is wise, if you are in such a scheme, for you to inform them of where you would like the money to go if you do die prematurely by filling in an 'expression of wish' form. This is especially sensible if you have a partner to whom you are not married. It could save delays and financial distress if they are reliant upon your earnings.

If your employers do not run a 'death in service' scheme, then your dependants may just get a lump sum equivalent to a refund of your and your employer's contributions with or without interest added. If you are in a money purchase scheme, your beneficiaries may be entitled to the value of your fund at death.

If you are in a final salary scheme and you die after retiring, then your spouse may be entitled to continue getting two-thirds of your pension until they die. But if you are in a money purchase scheme, then it will depend on the type of annuity you bought with your pension fund. (See Chapter Seven for further details about selecting annuities.)

Checklist
How good is your company final salary pension scheme?
   The perfect scheme would be one that gave you:

- Two-thirds final salary pension from the occupational scheme
- Fully inflation-proofed pension
- Full basic state pension, i.e. it is not discounted by your company pension
- Full SERPS pension, i.e. the occupational scheme has not contracted-out of SERPS, leaving your SERPS pension intact, or allowing you the choice of contracting-out personally
- Two-thirds pension for permanent incapacity before retirement, increasing by 5% p.a.
- Lump sum equal to four years' pay for widow/er for death in service, i.e. dying before you start drawing your pension
- Pension of 4/9ths of pay for widow/er for death in service, plus 1/8th of pension for dependent children
- Two-thirds of pension for widow/er after retirement
- Generous arrangements for early leavers

However, few employees are offered this Shangri-La. In the real world, you can count yourself lucky if you get half these features!

CHAPTER FOUR:
GETTING PERSONAL

Half of the working population are in jobs which do not offer them the chance to obtain a company pension. They therefore need to take charge of their own retirement planning. In the past this could prove quite a headache as the investment products available were relatively inflexible, but since 1 July 1988 it has been a much easier proposition. 1 July 1988 was the date when the Thatcher government introduced personal pension plans. This was heralded by the media and industry alike as something of a revolution. It was not that the product itself was revolutionary, indeed it was developed from the old self-employed pension plans, but for the first time people had a choice. No longer were employees locked into company pension schemes which might not be to their best advantage.

The personal pension plan is in many ways an investor's dream product. It is the most tax-efficient long-term savings plan available. It gives employees the chance to make regular savings net of basic rate tax to produce a lump sum and an income on retirement. Higher rate tax payers can claim back the difference between the two rates and the self-employed can claim back tax relief on their annual tax return. The savings within the plan are not taxed, unlike many other forms of savings, and when you retire you have the chance, subject to the existing tax rules, to take some of the money as a tax-free lump sum. Anyone who has net relevant earnings, and is not in a company pension or over age seventy-four is now able to invest in a personal pension.

The idea is that you can build up a pension fund throughout your working life regardless of how many different companies you have worked for. When you decide to retire you can use your savings to produce an income for life. How much you have depends on two things – how much you invest and how well your pension fund is invested. Obviously, the earlier you start the faster your fund will grow.

A personal pension has many advantages:

- You can choose how much you want to invest and can vary your premiums
- Your contributions are eligible for tax relief and you can make payments in respect of unused relief for previous years
- Your pension fund rolls up tax free
- If you are employed you can currently claim an incentive bonus from the Department of Social Security to add to your own contributions
- Your employer may be persuaded to contribute as well
- It is portable
- You can take the benefits at any time you want to after the age of fifty
- You can draw a lump sum from it when you take the benefits
- If you already have a retirement annuity (an old-style personal pension) in your investment portfolio, you can add a personal pension to give you extra flexibility, but be careful if you're a higher earner
- If you are in a company pension scheme and also have

earnings from another source, then you can use these
earnings as a basis for your own personal pension
- You can choose how your money is invested
- You can add on life cover and get tax relief on the
premiums you pay for it

Paying contributions

You can decide how much you want to pay and when
you want to pay your contributions. You can choose to
pay monthly or annually, single contributions or a
mixture. If you decide to pay regular amounts monthly or
annually your pension company can arrange for you to
build in provision for annual increases in your contributions so that they keep pace with the anticipated
increase in your earnings. This is quite important
because your fund will grow faster and, as you get older,
your pay is likely to increase above the level of inflation.
Besides, your standard of living is likely to improve as
you get older and most people like to maintain a similar
lifestyle when they retire. You will probably discover
that what seemed an adequate target when you started
your plan does not look quite so good later on. It is
therefore important to review your pension plan every
year or so to ensure that you are on course. You may
prefer to contribute to your pension fund every so often,
perhaps when you get a profit share from your employers
or windfall money. Indeed, if you are self-employed,
your earnings may be irregular and this option will give
you the flexibility you require.

Even if you start off with a regular payment plan, most
companies will allow you to add single contributions
from time to time. Indeed, many will also let you vary
your payment patterns without any penalty. You can
increase, decrease, stop or restart your contributions
almost at will. This facility is helpful for a number of
reasons. For example, if you have a career break to bring

up the children or to look after a sick relation, you do not have to worry about keeping up your contributions while you are not earning. Or, if you are approaching retirement or are temporarily earning extra cash, then you might want to syphon some more income into the plan in order to reap the rewards later. The government encourages older people especially to increase their contributions as they get closer to retirement by allowing them to pay even more in. You might also become unemployed, perhaps through redundancy or illness, and may not be able to keep up your payments. On the other hand, you might take a job which offers a really great pension scheme. In any of these cases you can arrange with the insurance company to stop contributing to your personal pension and leave the money invested.

Naturally, it will not be as good as if you had kept up your payments, but you do not lose the gains made and the chance for further gains. Then, if you find that you can afford to restart your contributions, you can usually do so. However, you should check that the insurance company will allow you this flexibility before you start your plan.

Tax relief on contributions
If you are employed, your contributions are paid net of basic rate tax. So if you are a basic rate taxpayer, for every £75 you contribute, you are credited with £100. This is easily done because the insurance company reclaims the tax from the Inland Revenue. If, however, you pay higher rate tax at 40% then you are credited with £100 for every £75 invested and have to claim the other £15 per £100 direct from the Inland Revenue. You will need to submit Form PP120 to your local tax office to get your tax code changed or obtain a rebate. If you are self-employed or a partner, slightly different rules apply; you claim your contributions against tax at your highest rate

by submitting Form PP120 with your annual tax return.

The Inland Revenue annually reviews the maximum contributions that you can pay at different ages into your personal pension. These percentages are different from those for people who are still contributing to the old-style self-employed retirement annuities, which could not be sold after 30 June 1988.

However, people who are still contributing to the old-style plan can use the extra tax relief to invest in a personal pension plan, provided they are aged thirty-six or over.

Table I: **Maximum contributions allowable against tax 1991–92**

Age*	Net relevant earnings (%)		
	Personal pension plan – new style	Retirement annuity – (Section 226) old style	Allowance available to Section 226 holders for personal pension
35 or less	17.5%	17.5%	nil
36–45	20.0%	17.5%	2.5%
46–50	25.0%	17.5%	7.5%
51–55	30.0%	20.0%	10.0%
56–60	35.0%	22.5%	12.5%
61–74	40.0%	27.5%	12.5%
75+	nil	nil	nil
Life cover**	5.0%	5.0%	n/a

* At start of year of assessment
** Included in the above percentages (see Life Cover, page 94)

There is another, overriding restriction on how much you can contribute to a personal pension because of something called the 'earnings cap', also known as the 'pensions cap'. This is set annually in the budget and is expected to be increased in line with inflation. The pensions cap for 1991–92 is £71,400. This means, for example, that the maximum a forty-five-year-old can contribute to his personal pension in 1991–92 is £71,400 × 20% = £14,280. In turn, this rule has implications for how much you can contribute to a new-style personal pension if you also have an old-style retirement annuity.

Example A:
Alan, aged fifty-one, earns £100,000 a year. He is contributing the maximum 20% (£20,000) to his retirement annuity contract. He wants to increase his contributions through a personal pension in which the maximum he can contribute is £21,420 (30% of the pensions cap of £71,400). As he is already paying £20,000 he can invest £1,420 in a personal pension.

George is fifty and earns £2,000 more than Alan, i.e. £102,000. He is contributing his maximum 17.5% (£17,850) to his retirement annuity. He cannot top this up with a personal pension because the most he can contribute in total is £17,850. Of course, he could spread the £17,850 between his retirement annuity and a new personal pension.

Whatever type of personal pension you have you can utilise unused relief from previous years to boost your pension fund, if you have enough money to spare! You do this by taking advantage of something called the 'carry forward' rule. This allows you to carry forward to this year up to six years unused relief, using the earliest years first. You can also 'carry back', by having a contribution treated as though it had been paid in the previous year, so that in effect you can claim unused relief for a maximum of seven years. However, first you have to have paid the maximum permissible contributions this year. You get tax relief at the current rate, not that prevailing in the year for which you are claiming unused relief. Therefore, if you are claiming this year against unused relief for 1985–86 when basic tax was 30% and the top rate was 60%, you will only be allowed tax relief at the current rates in 1991-92 when basic rate tax is 25% and the top rate is 40%.

Example B:
When James Spencer left the firm he was working with in March 1988, he was forty-three. He started a personal pension (not contracted-out) on 1 July 1988 when they were launched. He has made his maximum contribution of £5,000 this year, but finds he has some spare cash and wants to use up his unused relief for previous years. This is how he works out how much he is entitled to pay:

Tax year	Age	Earnings	Tax relief limits		Actual contri- butions	Unused relief
		£	%	£	£	£
1988–89	43	15,000	17.5	2,625	2,000	625
1989–90	44	16,000	20.0	3,200	3,000	200
1990–91	45	18,000	20.0	3,600	3,000	600
1991–92	46	20,000	25.0	5,000	5,000	—
James can contribute an extra:						1,425

If James can only afford to contribute £1,000 he has to wipe clean the early part of the slate first. This means he can carry forward £425 from year 1990–91 which he must use before 1997–98 or he loses it forever.

Fund rolls up tax free

Pension plans offer significantly better returns than any other form of saving for retirement. Most other savings plans suffer from tax on any income they earn, even if it is re-invested. However, with a personal pension, almost every penny the fund managers make is tax free. This means that your cash has the potential to grow faster. So, investors not only get tax relief on their contributions, but they also escape tax of 25% on any income that the fund attracts from its investments. That gives all pension funds a significant in-built advantage over any comparable investment. Further, you can take up to 25% of the fund as a tax free cash sum instead of pension, although whether or not that is advisable will be discussed in Chapter Seven.

SERPS rebate

A SERPS rebate pension can be a very attractive facility for younger people, in particular men under forty-five and women under thirty-eight. Young people in their late teens or early twenties have by far the most to gain from a personal pension with a good insurance company because their fund has longer to grow.

If you are earning more than £52 a week and are not in a company pension scheme, then you can contract-out of SERPS and use the money 'saved' to invest in your own personal pension. If you are in a company scheme which has not contracted-out, then you can still contract-out personally and run your own personal pension plan alongside your company scheme.

The state pension scheme for employees comprises two main payments:

● The basic state pension which is currently (1991–92) £52 a week (£2,704 p.a.), plus an allowance for a spouse which is currently £31.25 (£1,625 p.a.)

● SERPS, the State Earnings Related Pension, which is related to your earnings since 1978

Both of these pensions are inflation-proofed and can be expected to hold their buying power. The decision on whether to opt out of SERPS depends on whether you are convinced that your favoured insurance company will offer you a better return for your money in the long term than the state.

Qualifying for the basic state pension is merely a question of paying your basic National Insurance contributions for enough years (see Chapter Two).

You pay for the basic state pension from the 2% contributions you make on the first part of your earnings, currently £52 a week (£2,704 p.a.). If you are working and currently earning more than £52 you have no option but to pay this 2% (£1.04 a week) towards your basic state pension. Qualifying for your SERPS pension is another matter. If you are in a company scheme which is contracted-in, then you have the choice of whether to continue contributing to it or to divert your contributions to your own personal pension, called a rebate only personal pension. What happens is that some of the National Insurance contributions you pay in excess of the 2% for your basic pension, i.e. the 9% on earnings between £52 and £390 a week, helps you qualify for your SERPS pension. It is from this tranche of your National Insurance contributions that you can get a rebate to pay into your own appropriate personal pension. This is known as 'contracting-out' and it may enable you to secure a higher pension than you would have done by remaining in SERPS. Broadly speaking, the younger you are and the higher the real rate of return you expect to get from your plan, the greater the advantages of contracting-out. It is generally agreed that men up to their mid-forties and women up to their late thirties will probably do

better by contracting-out, provided that pension investments maintain a reasonable level of growth and continue to exceed the increase in national earnings by a
reasonable margin.

Once the incentive (an extra 2% introduced by the
government to encourage contracting-out) is scrapped in
1993, the age at which it would appear to be sensible not
to opt out will probably decrease by a couple of years.
However, whatever age you are, you should consider
your circumstances and get an opinion on your particular case.

If you wish to contract-out you can get a National
Insurance rebate of 5.8% of your 'band earnings' – that is
everything you earn above the Lower Earnings Level of
£52 a week (£2,704 p.a.) and below the Upper Earnings
Level of £390 a week (£20,280 p.a.) The 5.8% comprises
the 2% of your band earnings that you actually pay, plus
the 3.8% that your employer contributes. In addition,
until 5 April 1993, you can get a 2% incentive bonus.
This makes a total of 7.8% of band earnings, which
attracts a basic rate tax rebate of .66% (on your basic
contribution), bringing the total amount of money you
can pay into a personal pension to 8.46%.

Table J: SERPS Rebate

Actual earnings £	Rebate (premium) annually £	Available monthly £
8,000	448	37
10,000	617	51
12,000	786	65
14,000	955	79
16,000	1,143	95
18,000	1,293	107
20,280+	1,486	123

Notes:
1. Includes basic rate tax relief of .66% on employee's basic share of the rebate
2. Employees who leave a contracted-out company pension scheme without leaving the firm, having been members for more than two years, are not eligible for a rebate
3. Valid until April 1993

Source: Sun Life, 1991

Using the SERPS rebate to contract-out has some long-term conditions, which may or may not suit you. Some of the state pension rights which you have given up to 'go private' must be protected under a rule called 'Protected Rights'. Protected rights conditions are:

● You cannot take the protected rights part of your pension until you reach the state pension age. If you have made additional contributions you can draw a pension based on that part of your fund at any time after age fifty, but *not* from the contracted-out (protected rights) part. This means, for example, that if your total contributions are double the rebate, you will be able to draw half your fund out at fifty and convert that into an annuity but you will have to leave the other half until you reach the state pension age. Of course, the remainder of the fund will continue to be invested

● You cannot draw a lump sum from the SERPS rebate part of your pension fund as you can from a plain personal pension or an occupational scheme. However, you can draw a lump sum from the pension fund built up with any extra money you contribute. This means that if your total contributions are double the rebate you have received, you can draw a lump sum of 25% of half the fund, i.e. 12.5% of the total

- Once you start drawing your pension it must be increased by a minimum of 3% a year, or the Retail Prices Index if lower. On your death a continuing pension must be provided for your spouse (if you have one) provided he or she is aged forty-five or more, or has a dependent child. This is all done with the best intentions but you may prefer the choice of a level payment annuity
- Protected rights offer you no protection if your contracted-out pension turns out to be worse than SERPS would have been. The government will not make up the difference

Time is running out for people wishing to contract-out and get the incentive bonus. The decision to opt out for a particular year must be made before 5 April in that year as the system only deals in full tax years. The bonus will not be available after 5 April 1993. The rebates will be reviewed every five years and the government will indicate the new levels for the following five years. This should make it easier to plan ahead.

If you decide to contract-out then you must place all the rebate in a single plan. However, there is nothing to prevent you setting up another personal pension for other contributions which does not have the same rules. In fact, you can have as many personal pensions as you like provided you keep within the contribution limits laid down by the Inland Revenue (see Table I, page 80). You can contribute to any number of different plans in any one year – which wouldn't be very sensible because of the management charges involved. Or, you can start a plan with a different company every year or so. Some financial advisers recommend a good spread of plans, but it will clearly save management charges if you find a good company and stay with it. On the other hand you might decide that another company's plan is more appealing. You can even transfer your personal pension funds from one pension company to another. If you wish to consider doing this then you can ask your pension provider for a transfer value, which will vary according to investment conditions and any transfer charges levied. Under normal circumstances this is not to be recommended as you will be penalised for moving. Indeed, in early years the transfer value may be less than the total contributions you have paid, just as the surrender value of a life assurance policy in the early years is usually less than your contributions.

It is important to accept that it is highly unlikely that just using your rebate money, probably around 6% of earnings between something like £52 and £390 a week, will be enough to provide you with a decent pension. It is far better to add new money to it, preferably from the outset because the longer the money is in the fund the longer it has to grow. If you are lucky you might find that by age fifty you really do have enough money to retire on. If you don't want to retire then you can stop contributing and let the fund continue to grow.

Your employer can contribute

If you are employed, but not in the company pension scheme, and you decide to take out a personal pension you can ask your employer to contribute to it, whether it is a contracted-out plan or an ordinary one. The total contributions from you and your employer must not, however, exceed the maximum limits shown in Table I, page 80).

Employers tend to be rather protective about their final salary schemes, so if they run one they may prefer not to contribute to your scheme.

Portable pensions
Portability is one of the marvellous advantages of personal pensions. It is a great plus for people who can expect to change their jobs a few times in their career, for example those working in publishing, advertising, the leisure industry, the hotel trade, motor sales and the construction industry. Personal pensions really come into their own for women who are far more likely to change jobs because of enforced career breaks, perhaps to bring up the children or look after sick relations.

Company final salary pension schemes should carry a wealth warning for job swappers. People who change jobs tend to put in too little time with each firm to build up a decent pension and leave a trail of pension rights behind which will be less than if they had stayed with one employer, all else being equal. Table E (page 65) shows the effect on pension benefits of moving jobs.

If you always work for companies with money purchase schemes, then you get some protection as the money that has built up is earmarked for you and should keep growing after you have left. However, you cannot always be sure that in future all your employers will have a money purchase scheme.

It is sometimes possible to draw your money out of previous employers' pension schemes and put it into a buy-out bond or a personal pension of your own. If you have had a number of jobs and have been in the company final salary schemes, it is sensible to investigate the chances of doing that (see Chapter Three). However, in future or if you are starting out on your career, you might do better to settle for a personal pension if you expect to make a few job changes over the years. You can continue to invest in your personal pension regardless of who employs you – or indeed, even if you become self-employed.

Retirement at fifty

You will have to wait until you reach the statutory retirement age (sixty for women and sixty-five for men) before you can draw any state pensions, but you can start drawing the new-style personal pensions at any time from age fifty (or even earlier if you're in serious ill-health). If you have a contracted-out plan then you cannot draw that portion which is based on your SERPS contributions. If you have an old-style retirement annuity you cannot start drawing it until you are sixty, although you can transfer it to a personal pension. Also, you could take benefits earlier if you are in serious ill-health.

Many people wish to retire from their main career in their fifties. They sometimes want to try a new career or set up their own business. By the time you are in your fifties you should have a clear idea of whether you will have sufficient pension to live comfortably on. If you wish to take on another job and therefore have some income from another source, you may decide not to draw your pension, or only to draw part of it. Just knowing that you have enough reserves to retire on may well give you the confidence to try something new.

Most personal pension plans are devised in such a way that they are split into a cluster of ten policies so that you can draw your pension in ten stages. If you do this you can draw off a tax-free lump sum of up to 25% from each policy if you wish. By adopting this strategy, the rest of your fund held under the remaining policies has the chance to grow giving you a bigger potential pension for later. You can even continue contributing to it provided that you are still earning and do not breach the maximum contribution rules (see Table I, page 80).

If you are seriously incapacitated you can sometimes start drawing your personal pension before you are fifty. You will have to ask your pension provider for details. Also, if you belong to a special category, you may be allowed to draw your personal pension early. The following table shows whom the Inland Revenue allows to retire early and start drawing their new-style personal pension or the old-style self-employed pension:

Table K: **MINIMUM RETIREMENT AGES**

Profession or occupation	Retirement age
Air pilots	55*
Athletes (appearance and prize money only)	35
Badminton players	35
Boxers	35
Brass instrumentalists	55*
Circus animal trainers	50
Cricketers	40
Croupiers	50
Cyclists (professional)	35
Dancers	35
Distant water trawlermen	55*
Divers (saturation, deep sea and free swimming)	40
Firemen (part-time)	55*
Footballers	35
Golfers (tournament earnings)	40
Inshore fishermen	55*
Inter dealer brokers	50
Jockeys – flat racing	45
– national hunt	35
Martial art instructors	50
Models	35
Moneybroker dealers (excluding directors and managers responsible for dealers)	50
Moneybroker dealers (directors and managers responsible for dealers)	55*

Motorcycle riders (motocross or road racing)	**40**
Motor racing drivers	**40**
Newscasters (ITV)	**50**
Nurses, physiotherapists, midwives or health visitors who are females	**55***
Off-shore riggers	**50**
Psychiatrists (who are also maximum part-time specialists employed in the NHS solely in the treatment of the mentally disordered)	**55***
Royal Marine Reservists (non-commissioned)	**45**
Royal Naval Reservists	**50**
Rugby League players	**35**
Rugby League referees	**50**
Singers	**55***
Speedway riders	**40**
Squash players	**35**
Tennis players (including Real Tennis)	**35**
Territorial Army members	**50**
Trapeze artists	**40**
Wrestlers	**35**

* People with old-style retirement annuities can retire at fifty if they transfer to a new-style personal pension. (See below: old-style versus new-style personal pensions)

Lump sum

If you have a new-style personal pension you can draw a tax-free lump sum of 25% of the fund, excluding the Protected Rights portion which was financed by your SERPS rebate. If you take a lump sum then you reduce the amount of money you can turn into an income, unless you reinvest the cash yourself for income.

Those of you with an old-style retirement annuity have to follow different rules. These say that generally the maximum lump sum you can draw is three times the remaining pension after the cash has been withdrawn. This figure is difficult to quantify because it is tied to prevailing annuity rates at the time you make the decision. However, it usually works out to more than a quarter of the fund. The older you are, the larger it is and men get more than women of the same age. Another rule says that if you started contributing to a retirement annuity on or after 17 March 1987, the maximum lump sum you can draw is £150,000. People with personal pensions suffer no such limitations – they can draw 25% regardless of how much is left.

Old-style versus new-style personal pensions
This brings us to a comparison between old-style retirement annuities and the new style personal pension. If you have an old-style pension is it worth your while converting it, usually for a minimal adminstrative charge, into a new-style pension?

- If you want to retire, or start drawing your pension before you are sixty, then you will need to convert your policy to a new-style plan
- If your main priority is to be able to draw the largest tax-free lump sum, then you would generally be better off staying put. If you have a pre-March 1987 retirement annuity plan and you plan to work after normal retirement age, then it will increasingly pay you to stay put. However, if you have a post-March 1987 retirement annuity and your fund is likely to be in excess of £600,000, then you should consider conversion
- If you are employed, but not in a company contracted-out pension, then you can use a personal pension plan to contract out personally and get the SERPS rebate. You cannot use an old-style pension plan to contract out

- Pin-money pension. If you have a money-making sideline and are in a company pension scheme then you are also normally allowed to contribute to a personal pension based on your freelance earnings. The amount that you can contribute is limited to the appropriate percentage of your (freelance) earnings for your age (see Table I, page 80)
- If you are a higher earner and have an old-style retirement annuity, your contributions will not be restricted by the earnings cap considerations. If you convert it to a new contract, they will

Disadvantage of personal pensions

The disadvantage of a personal pension for employees who decide not to join the company pension scheme is that they often lose out on life cover. Many companies offer life assurance and sickness benefits for their employees only if they are in the company pension scheme. This is a valuable benefit because a benefit package attached to a pension scheme could:

- Pay up to two-thirds of your salary to you if you are so seriously incapacitated because of an accident or through ill-health that you cannot carry on working
- Pay out a lump sum of up to four years salary to your dependants if you die while still working for the firm but before retirement
- Pay out a spouse's pension of up to two-thirds of your earnings if you die in service

However, you can fill in some of the gaps by including life cover under your personal pension. Whatever type of personal pension you have you are allowed to get full tax relief, at your highest rate of tax, on life assurance premiums of up to 5% of your normal earnings. This 5% comes out of the appropriate limits on contributions to

94

personal pensions for your age allowed by the Inland Revenue. You can have life cover to leave your dependants with a lump sum as long as you hold the plan. It may be a good idea to write it in Trust. If you want protection in the case of being incapacitated and unable to work then you should consider paying for a 'waiver of premium benefit'. This may cost an extra 5% or so of your contribution, but it means that if you are unable to work you stop contributing to your pension and the insurance company contributes instead, so that your pension does not suffer.

Self-administered personal pension schemes
It is possible for you to set up your own self-administered personal pension scheme, in which you select your own investments, rather than rely on the traditional pre-packaged with-profits or unit-linked investments that form the basis of most personal pensions. They could be really exciting and challenging to administer, but this is a highly specialised area.

These schemes require Inland Revenue approval before you can go ahead, and then once they are set up the Inland Revenue tends to monitor them closely. Also, you will almost certainly need the advice of a very experienced financial adviser who specialises in such schemes to ensure that you conform to the rules and, more importantly, that the money will be there when you want to retire.

These schemes are not to be recommended to anyone who hasn't got the right professional expertise or the money to buy in the quality of advice that is necessary to prevent the scheme ending in disaster and/or perpetual correspondence with the Inland Revenue.

CHAPTER FIVE:
YOUR CHOICE

Any number of financial organisations can provide your personal pension plan. While most are provided by the insurance companies and the unit trust companies, a number of financial management companies including banks and building societies also offer personal pensions. But banks and building societies which offer personal pension plans are not usually investing the money for you, unless you select a deposit-based plan (see page 101), instead they are acting as agents for an insurance company.

It is also necessary to understand that there is a major difference between investing in a pension fund and drawing your pension. First of all you build up your fund, which you can do with a number of authorised companies, and then you use the money to buy your annuity which can only be provided by an insurance company. You can, however, make arrangements to draw your money through the building society and bank with whom you invested your money in the first place, but they are not actually providing the money.

Therefore, during the life of your pension plan you have to make two basic, but major, purchasing decisions:

● From whom to buy your pension plan
● From whom to buy your annuity

You can ask your favourite insurance company or financial adviser for advice, to help you narrow the field. In this chapter we explain how to choose a financial adviser, but first of all we will look at the alternative types of pension plan you can buy. Although we talk about personal pensions throughout the chapter, most of the considerations also apply to executive pension plans, which are covered in more detail in Chapter Six.

When you start looking for a personal pension plan you will find a bewildering range of choice and lots of people keen to advise you. It pays to remember that there is no such thing as the best personal pension plan for everyone. There is a great deal of competition for personal pension business and companies are always trying to improve their contracts. They usually do this by offering investors greater flexibility. The art of pension planning is to find a contract that offers you exactly what you want.

The following thirteen-point checklist should help you make your decisions. We will go through each point in turn explaining its relevance:

● The need for good investment performance
● Types of plan (with-profits versus unit-linked) and assessment of past investment performance
● Choosing between with-profits and unit-linked
● Can you switch between funds easily and cheaply
● Can you stop, start and vary your contributions easily and without penalty
● Can automatic increases be built into contributions
● Can you have a waiver of premiums if you become too ill to work
● Can you easily arrange a loan against the fund if you hit a financial crisis
● Can you retire early without penalty
● Can you phase in your pension over a number of years

- Is life cover available with the plan
- If you die before retirement will your dependants get all your fund returned to them
- Is the plan easy to read

The need for good investment performance

The most important requirement for a pension fund is that it grows so well that there will be sufficient money when you retire to provide you with a reasonable income. The same rules apply to all types of pension.

Obviously, the size of your pension depends partly on how much you contribute, so it is not worth short-changing yourself. As a guideline, we suggest that by investing 10% of your earnings you should produce a satisfactory pension. If you discover in your mid-forties or fifties that your fund is not growing fast enough, then you can consider taking advantage of the increased maximum contributions for older people in order to increase your contributions.

It is very important to get advice or to do some research, since the difference between the best and worst companies is enormous. The worst performing company could leave you with a pension fund worth half the value of the best.

Types of plan

— With-profits

With-profits pension plans are only managed by life assurance companies, although they may be sold through bank and building societies. With-profits pension plans are a version of the familiar old endowment policies or the low-cost endowment policies with which you may be financing the purchase of your house. Your contributions are added to other people's contributions in the fund and invested in a broad range of investments.

This may include shares, government stocks, property and money markets.

The value of your pension will depend on the company's investment performance and the attitude of its actuary. Every year the company actuary works out how much profit has been made on the fund's investments. He adds the income received from the investments to the increase in their value over the year and allocates a share of this to the with-profits policyholders. He will not allocate all the money. Some is held back for the company's reserves and to pay benefits at a later date. When he has decided on the allocation, he will declare an annual bonus, called a reversionary bonus. The company will add this sum to your pension fund. Once this is done it can never be deducted and future bonuses will be calculated on the increased value of the fund. As well as annual bonuses, there are special so-called 'terminal' bonuses added when the benefits are taken.

— *Unit-linked*

There are special unit-linked investment funds which are authorised to be used for pension plans. There is no tax on any income or profits they produce. You can buy them from insurance companies, friendly societies and unit trust companies. In unit-linked pension plans you do not get the cushioning effect you get in with-profits plans because your contributions, less management charges, are used to buy units in the chosen fund. The value of your fund when you retire depends on the value of your units at that time. This means if the stock market is doing badly on the day you want to cash in your fund to buy your pension, then the value of your fund will be depressed. This is because the price of your units varies from day to day and therefore changes the value of your fund.

If the prices are down, then the money available to buy

your pension will be reduced and your pension will suffer. You may be able to wait for conditions to improve and delay the time at which you start drawing your pension; on the other hand, of course, the stock market may be very buoyant and it may be a very good time to sell.

Companies which provide unit-linked pension plans usually offer a wide selection of funds from which to choose. This may be a mixed blessing, depending on how familiar you are with investments or how good your financial adviser is when recommending the funds you should select. One advantage with unit-linked plans is that you can switch your investments from one fund to another. Typically, you get one free switch a year and have to pay for any others.

Funds are usually arranged in sectors. For example, you can choose to invest all or some of your money in United Kingdom equities (shares in UK companies), in European companies, in Pacific companies, in a broad range of international shares or in property. All these sectors carry varying degrees of risk, i.e. the risk that your money might fall in value. However, all unit-linked pension plan managers offer one managed or general fund which is designed to be less risky, but this fund may not build up very fast. Some offer funds invested in the absolutely safe government stocks, but you will be sacrificing potential growth for the added security. It may make sense as you near retirement age to switch the bulk of your savings into these.

— Unitised with-profits

Unitised with-profits pension plans are a sort of half-way house between with-profits and unit-linked plans. You buy units in a with-profits fund so that the value of your fund cannot fall and every year you are allocated a bonus depending on the performance of the fund. The bonus increases the value of your units and you should qualify for a terminal bonus when you retire. Only insurance companies are allowed to offer unitised with-profits pension plans, though you can buy them through banks and building societies. They were only introduced in the mid-1980s so their track record is too short to provide a sound basis for assessment.

— Deposit-based plans

Deposit-based or deposit administration plans are basically high interest deposit accounts offered by some insurance companies, building societies and banks. As you cannot withdraw the money until you start drawing your pension, which means they expect your money to remain invested for some years, these offer a higher rate of interest than normal accounts. The interest earned is tax free and the fund builds up faster than if you left the cash in a bank account from which tax is deducted. They are risk free because the value of your capital cannot fall. However, in the long term, they are unlikely to give you as good a result as more risky forms of pension plan.

The main use for this type of plan is to protect the value of your pension fund in the last two or three years before you expect to retire. If, for example, you have a unit-linked pension plan and have made some good gains, you can transfer your money to one of these cash-type funds. Some pension companies do it automatically if you ask them. This will protect your profits while still adding some valuable interest. Usually you will find that when the stock market is depressed interest rates tend to rise and conversely when the stock market is buoyant interest rates tend to decrease.

With-profits versus unit-linked

It has become fashionable for investors to be persuaded to buy unit-linked plans instead of the traditional with-profits plans. There are two schools of thought about this. With-profits are considered safer because once the bonuses have been allocated they cannot be taken away. Unit-linked plans are considered more risky as there are no guarantees on their value at retirement. The school that favours with-profits points out some very good and consistent results from the leading life assurance companies, saying that while unit-linked funds may and sometimes do outperform the best with-profits plans, there are more consistently reliable with-profits plans than unit-linked plans. Also, that the odds of picking the right unit-linked fund are stacked against you. Anyone whose unit-linked plan matured just after the United Kingdom stock-market crash of 1987 might agree!

The pro unit-linked school argues that the with-profits plans suffer from their innate conservatism by including the more pedestrian fixed-interest and less exciting equities, that you have to take a bit of a risk and that the closer your investment is to mainline equities (i.e. the Stock Exchange), historically the bigger your ultimate fund will be. Anyone whose unit-linked plan matured just before the UK stock market crash of 1987 might agree with this school of thought.

The undecided school suggests that you could compromise between the two and either select a unitised with-profits fund or at least put some of your money into such a fund and the rest elsewhere. Alternatively, you could divide your contributions between a full-blooded with-profits plan and a more exciting unit-linked fund. This leaves the deposit-based schemes. In the short term they are considered very good for holding the value of your money and perhaps increasing your capital a little above the rate of inflation. However, they are not advised for anyone bar the very timid or those nearing retirement who wish to lock in their gains, as the long term growth potential is poor.

Flexibility

In the lifetime of a personal pension fund, which may be up to forty-five years, many things can happen on the world stage that may influence your approach to investing. Eastern Europe might take off, so might China, or exciting new developments might occur in the energy sector. Therefore, you should consider at the outset what flexibility is built into your choice. Even if you choose a with-profits plan you can arrange a transfer to another plan or even another company. You should ask the company when you take out the plan whether they will penalise you for doing this; some companies will not. If you buy a unit-linked pension plan it is important to check that you have the facility to switch between the various funds at a reasonable cost; some charge you for this, others allow one or two free switches a year.

Can you stop, start and vary your contributions easily and without penalty?

Before you take out a pension plan you should decide how often you wish to make contributions – monthly, annually or occasionally, or any combination of the three. If you have a regular income you may prefer to pay monthly, with the option of adding extra money occasionally. For example, towards the end of the tax year you may want to use up more of the contribution which you are allowed to make, but you do not want to be committed to doing this every year. If your employers are contributing they would almost certainly prefer you to have a monthly contract. If you are self-employed you may also prefer a flexible arrangment so you can base your decision on each year's profit.

At some stage in your working life you may want to stop your contributions for a while. You might get a job which offers an absolutely super pension scheme or you may stop working altogether because of redundancy or illness. Women have to take into account the prospect of career breaks to bring up children or to look after ailing relations. It is therefore sensible to make sure that you can stop, start or vary your contributions easily and without penalty.

If you choose to pay monthly premiums, check the minimum number of payments required. Different companies have different rules, but most will insist on you paying the contributions for at least one year and some have minimum monthly payment levels. Although it is easy to stop contributing to a with-profits plan, you need to be sure it will continue to grow and attract bonuses until you wish to draw your pension. As not all companies will add the extra money, it's well worth a check.

Can automatic increases be built into contributions?
A sensible arrangement, if you are making regular contributions, is to build in some increases as you earn more money. Quite a number of companies now ask you if you wish your contributions to increase automatically each year by a certain percentage such as the Retail Prices Index or the Average Earnings Index. This saves you from the trouble of having to write to them every time you have a pay rise and ask them to increase your contributions. It also helps to ensure that your fund will increase in line with your increased earnings.

Can you have a waiver of premiums if you become too ill to work?
One potentially valuable option, which may cost an extra 2% to 3%, is the waiver of contributions. This means that if you become too ill to work for any reason (excluding conditions such as alcoholism or drug addiction) the company will keep up your contributions at the level they were immediately prior to your illness. If you had

built in automatic increases in contributions they will possibly increase their contributions at the higher rate. They will pay this money up to your return to work, or even your normal retirement date if necessary. This protects your pension arrangements for your normal working lifetime.

Can you easily arrange a loan against the fund if you hit a financial crisis?

Some people are wary about contributing as much as they would wish to their personal pension because they cannot touch any of the money until they retire. Therefore, quite a number of companies will allow you to borrow against your fund in cases of emergency so that you do not feel that you have kissed the money goodbye until retirement age.

The rules restrict you to a certain percentage of the fund but the interest rates are usually quite good compared with, say a bank loan. In practice, very few people actually take out such loans but it can be useful in a crisis.

Is life cover available with the plan?

Some insurance companies offer you life cover as part of your pension plan, which means you are able to obtain tax relief on the premiums. You can take this option provided that the maximum you pay is 5% of your normal earnings and that, when added to your pension contributions, it does not exceed your maximum contribution. This can be a cheap way of getting term assurance to protect your dependants. It is a useful substitute for the life cover that people in occupational pension schemes often receive automatically.

Can you retire early without penalty?

A surprising number of plans penalise you for bringing

forward the date at which you wish to retire. They do this because they like to know exactly how long they are going to have your money in order to plan their investment strategy.

Unless you are very close to retiring, it is difficult to know when the actual date will be. There may be all sorts of reasons why you want to bring the date forward: illness, redundancy, or just because you feel like it. Besides, if you have a unit-linked contract and the stock market is doing incredibly well, you might want to pull out when you think your fund is at its peak without having to worry about the pension provider charging you. Therefore, if you have a choice of two similar plans that you like and one charges you for retiring early and the other one does not, you would be best advised to take the one that does not.

There is one alternative choice. If you really like a certain plan and the only flaw you can find is that it penalises you for early retirement, all you have to do to preserve your position is say that you want to retire at fifty (the earliest age). You can then retire whenever you want to after that date and it will make absolutely no difference to your position. You or your fund will not suffer as you will not be penalised for retiring late.

Can you phase in your pension over a number of years?
Being able to phase in your pension over a number of years, which means that you can cash in your fund in stages, could be quite useful. This facility, which is also known as the 'multiple plan facility', means that the contract is arranged so that your plan is in a cluster of ten policies. At its simplest, you can start drawing your pension in up to ten stages, or any suitable number of combinations, for example you may like to draw 7/10ths to start with and then add the other 3/10ths one at a time over a number of years. Each time you do this your lump

sum is adjusted accordingly, so that you can draw off a lump sum of 25% of the fraction of the fund you have cashed in. It may be an option that you do not wish to take up, but experience shows that people who have retired appreciate the choice. The circumstances under which you may use the option include:

- Retiring from your main job and taking a part-time job, but needing to top up your income, while preserving part of your fund intact and still with growth potential
- Retiring with a small company pension if, for instance, you have been an early leaver and want to keep part of your personal pension fund intact for a while
- You may want to build in an element of inflation-proofing and leave some of your fund still growing, even if you are not still contributing to it
- Your spouse or partner may still be working when you retire and you do not need to draw your full fund

If you die before retirement will your dependants get all your fund returned to them?
Most pension providers will pay the total of your fund to your estate if you die before you draw it, but some don't. There are four variations. Return of fund (ROF) is usually the best deal for the investor, as your estate gets a full return of fund which will be valued at the date of death. Return with interest (RWI) is next in the pecking order. This means that your estate gets the sum total of all your premiums with compound interest at a rate which should be stated in the plan literature. All growth in the fund is ignored. The only time when this would be the best buy would be if there had been a prolonged stock market recession and the value of shares had sunk. Return no interest (RNI), is much less favourable; your contributions are returned with no interest payable. This means

that your estate only gets your contributions back, which is a pretty poor deal unless the pension fund provider offers some extra concession that you may want, such as preferential annuity rates if you survive. No return (NR) is the worst possible deal; as its name suggests, your estate will receive nothing if you die before you start drawing your pension. Go into this type of contract with your eyes open. Make sure the benefits outweigh the disadvantages.

If you do have death-benefits under your plan, it could be a good idea to write them in Trust. The benefits can then fall outside your estate and will not be liable for Inheritance Tax.

Is the plan easy to read?
Beware of the glossy pension plan brochure that is complicated. If it is difficult to read you might miss some important details and find that what you thought you bought and what you actually bought are quite different. Most pension providers now make an effort to be clear and include a question and answer section. There is nothing wrong with this, but they might not answer *your* questions. If you have any questions that are important to you, or if there is anything you do not understand, do not hesitate to ask the company or your financial adviser to explain it to you in writing.

Financial strength of the company
Last, but by no means least, you ought to give some consideration to the quality of the company you are considering. When you select a company you want to be sure that it is well run and can produce consistently high investment performances. You also want to know that it has sufficient reserves to absorb dramas such as international stock markets taking a nose-dive. This is especially important if you have a with-profits policy

because you do not want to miss any annual bonus and you want a good terminal bonus when you cash in your fund. If you choose a unit-linked pension plan you will have to bear in mind that the fund managers cannot use their reserves to help you out.

How to choose a financial adviser
Having decided that you wish to go ahead and buy a personal pension and the main ingredients that you want it to have, you now have some more decisions to make. Which plan do you want and who are you going to buy it from? You have the choice of:

- Going direct to a company (or more than one) that you have discovered from the league tables has a very good investment track record. In this case you will deal with a company representative
- Going to an independent financial adviser (or more than one) and asking them to recommend a good plan for you that fulfils your requirements. They can recommend from all the companies in the marketplace
- Going to a financial adviser who is tied to a particular insurance company. They will have an in-depth knowledge of the products available from their company
- Going to your bank manager or building society manager and asking them to recommend a pension plan. As most banks and building societies are 'tied', which means that they have arranged to sell only one company's plans, it is much the same as going direct to an insurance or unit trust company
- Going to your accountant or solicitor. If they advise on personal finance they will be independent and free to recommend from all the companies in the marketplace

The meeting

Once you have decided who is going to give you financial advice, you need to do some preparation to define your requirements. Run the ruler over your finances so that you know where you stand. Establish how much you have invested, what your assets and debts are, what income you have now and what you expect to have; what insurance or pension arrangements you already have and how much you think you can afford to contribute to your pension. If you have all the details at your fingertips at the meeting, you will be able to concentrate on the answers to your questions rather than worrying about where you left your insurance policy documents. If you appear confident and organised you will get the best from the meeting. The sort of questions your adviser will need to ask are listed in the following checklist:

- Your current income and likely income
- Savings total
- Life policies, premiums and sums assured
- Tax position, tax number
- National Insurance number and note of any missing years such as career breaks
- Financial commitments such as mortgage, loans, private education for the children, or responsibility for dependants
- Other pension schemes you might have belonged to
- Your proposed retirement age
- Investment philosophy, i.e. cautious, realistic or adventurous
- State of health

Pension planning is quite complex and you will probably need several meetings, with the adviser of your choice before you come to any firm decisions. Remember, since your pension benefits may well benefit other members of your family, it pays to discuss your arrangements thoroughly with those likely to be affected and to review your overall life assurance and health cover plus any need for Inheritance Tax planning.

CHAPTER SIX:
EXECUTIVE OPTIONS

Company executives may have a number of types of pension scheme open to them, depending on the size of the company and whether the executives own the company. This chapter is written mainly with the directors of small businesses in mind. It is not intended as a definitive guide, but to sketch in some of the options that are available. Executive pensions are a very complex subject involving some potentially beneficial tax concessions and the possibility of borrowing against your pension fund to help the company. Therefore it is essential that you consult your accountant or financial adviser for their relevance to you and your company.

Approval of all company pension schemes is at the discretion of the Superannuation Funds Office. They require to be satisfied that the sole purpose of the plan is the provision of relevant benefits on retirement and death. However, there are a few ways for executives to achieve a good pension within the tax laws.

Basically, the options for employed executives running their own company include:

- Executive pension plans
- Small self-administered pension schemes (SSASs)
- Personal pensions

Executive pensions

At its simplest, an executive pension is a small occupational pension with only one member. It is a money purchase scheme, which builds up a fund that later provides your pension, but it has additional benefits which make it similar to other occupational schemes. It has to be an insured scheme, which means that it is provided by an authorised life assurance company although you might buy it from a bank or building society. Many members of executive pension arrangements or small self-administered schemes will be higher earners and the Inland Revenue has restrictions on how the salary of these employees and directors is calculated for pension purposes. Details are contained in Appendix Two.

As well as providing your retirement income, an insured pension scheme can include life cover such as death benefits so that your spouse and/or dependants get a lump sum of up to four times final salary as well as a pension of 4/9ths final salary if you die before you retire. An executive remuneration package could also include permanent health insurance so that if you become too ill to work you are guaranteed a minimum income until you reach your pension age, at which time you can start drawing your pension. If extra benefits like these are to be included, you may need to have a medical.

You can use this type of executive pension plan as part of your Inheritance Tax (IHT) planning, but it is essential to have professional advice. One major advantage is that death benefits from pension schemes are not normally subject to Inheritance Tax.

Another great advantage of executive pension plans is that, unlike personal pension schemes, you can, in effect, catch up on unlimited past years of service. For example, if you are an executive aged fifty-five running your own company, which is doing very well, and you have made no pension arrangements at all, your company may be able to make one large payment to cover contributions for all your past years of service. So, in one bound, you can catch up – if your company has enough money. Alternatively, your company can spread the payments for past years over future years by increased annual contributions. Any money that your company pays can normally be charged against profits for Corporation Tax purposes to reduce the burden on the company. The different rates at which you can accrue benefits are shown in Appendix Two.

However, you can also contribute up to 15% of your salary if you wish, and get income tax relief at your highest rate of tax. Legally, there is no requirement for you to make any contributions out of your personal earnings, but the facility is there if you wish to use it.

Being able, effectively, to buy past years like this makes executive pensions potentially better than personal pensions, depending on your individual circumstances and if your company can afford it, because with personal pensions you can only roll back your contributions for the previous seven years, and your contributions are limited to a certain level (see Chapter Four for further details).

To give you some idea of how much money you will need to invest in an executive pension let's assume, quite realistically, that you wish to pay annually, that you have sufficient past service with the company and you need an accumulated fund of ten times salary to provide the maximum pension. If you start the plan within three years of retirement, then clearly you will need to contribute something in excess of 300% of salary to hit the target. If you wish to take out such a plan, you will need to get a quote from an insurance company to establish how much money you will need to contribute in order to meet your retirement objectives.

Premiums will be based on a number of factors:

- Your age at entry
- Your sex
- Your current earnings
- The number of years before you expect to retire
- The amount of past service

They are increased if you wish to include three further popular options:

- Lump sum for your dependants if you die in service
- Spouse's pension
- Increasing pension

You will obviously not want to divert money away from your fund-building to secure the first two options if you are single and childless, or have no intention of getting married and starting a family.

It is important to realise that, while the scheme rules allow you to draw up to two-thirds final salary when you retire, if the fund is not sufficiently large you will not be able to do so. On the other hand, your fund might be so large that your ultimate pension will exceed the two-thirds limit. In that case, the trustees will have to decide what they will do with the surplus. Having a surplus is less likely for late starters but, if it looks like happening, you may be able to arrange for a larger spouse's pension on your death, or greater increases on your pension.

While most executive pension plans are set up by executives of small companies for themselves, they are also used to top up the pension arrangements of key personnel in established occupational schemes who cannot put in enough time to achieve a full two-thirds pension. Executive pension schemes can run in tandem with existing pension plans provided that the ultimate aggregate pension benefits are not going to exceed Inland Revenue limits.

Another major use for an executive pension is for a spouse employed in the business. For example, you may be the wife of a man in business on his own account or he may be in partnership with others and if you are working for the business, then your husband or the partners can establish an executive pension plan for you. Likewise, if you are running the business and your husband works for you, then you can set up an executive pension plan for him. Appendix Two gives full details of the benefit regimes which apply to existing executive pensions and you should consult your financial adviser for up-to-date information on the tax treatment of benefits.

Small Self-Administered Schemes (SSASs)

A SSAS gives you the freedom to invest (within Inland Revenue limits) where you choose. You don't have to limit yourself to the fund manager of the insurance company. You can invest directly in shares or property. The scheme can also lend money back to the company within certain constraints. Every small self-administered scheme must have a pensioneer trustee. This is a person or body widely involved with occupational pension schemes, who undertakes to ensure that if the scheme is wound up, this is done in accordance with the rules.

The managing trustees are usually the directors of the company involved and have wide-ranging investment powers, including loans to the company and purchase of commercial property to be leased to the company. This is a valuable facility because the SSAS can be used to assist with further development of the company as well as providing pension benefits later.

Let's suppose that the company contributes £100,000 to your pension scheme. The £100,000 is allowable as an expense when Corporation Tax is calculated and the scheme can lend the company up to 25% (£25,000) straightaway. In the third year of the scheme, this percentage can be increased to 50%. There are restrictions of course, like the company having to pay the pension fund a commercial rate of interest, typically three percentage points over base rate. You can't borrow money from the fund for personal use or that of your relations. For example, you cannot use it to pay for your children's private education, even if you do argue that that is a sound investment for the future of the company. Finally, all the members must be managing trustees if full advantage is to be taken of the investment opportunities.

The main tax advantages of an SSAS include:

- The company's contributions are an allowable expense against profits for Corporation Tax. Provided the scheme is approved by the Inland Revenue, these contributions are not treated as additional remuneration for the employee. Also, they do not attract National Insurance contributions
- If you make any personal contributions they can be set against your earnings and therefore income tax relief is obtained up to your highest rate of tax
- The investments grow free of United Kingdom tax on capital gains and investment income
- You can choose to take part of your retirement benefits in the form of a tax-free lump sum
- All benefits payable on your death before age seventy-five would normally be free of Inheritance Tax
- You have up to five years after retirement in which to pick the best time to buy your annuity with an insurance company. This could be most beneficial if stock market and money market conditions are unfavourable at the time of retirement. You can hold on until the market picks up or when annuity rates work in your favour

Having decided the initial level of contribution the company makes on your behalf it is not committed to that level. The company can increase or decrease future contributions (within the limits set by the Inland Revenue). Therefore contributions can be tailored to the company's changing circumstances. The Inland Revenue, through the Superannuation Funds Office (SFO) which oversees company pension schemes, would normally expect the level of the initial contribution to remain fairly constant for the first three years. If the contribution decreases significantly, there is a possibility that Corporation Tax relief can be spread over more than one accounting year.

As well as ensuring a good retirement income, you can build into the SSAS some protection for your family should you die prematurely or become so disabled that you are unable to carry on working. Typically this would mean that they get a lump sum equal to some four times your annual salary, plus a return of your contributions (with or without interest), plus a pension equal to two-thirds of what you would have got for your spouse. Again, you will probably need to provide medical evidence to obtain these benefits.

The following example shows how to use a SSAS to save your company money at the same time as making good arrangements for your retirement.

Example:
Executive aged 40

Salary	£20,280
Current company profits	£30,000
Amount available	£50,280

Personal details:
Married, two children, receives personal allowance and married couple's allowance
Husband owns 99% of company shares
Wife owns 1%

Calls and potential calls on money come from:
Corporation Tax
National Insurance
Inheritance Tax
Capital Gains Tax
PAYE

What can he do with the company profits?
He has the following main choices:
1) Retain in company, or
2) Pay as salary, or
3) Declare a dividend, or
4) Make a pension contribution
5) Part salary/part pension

Choice 1: Pay corporation tax

Profits	£30,000
Corporation Tax @ 25%	£ 7,500
Retain in company	£22,500

But retained money may be liable to Capital Gains Tax or Inheritance Tax @ 40%
Therefore:

£22,500 × 40% =	£ 9,000
plus Corporation Tax	£ 7,500
Total tax could be:	£16,500

Therefore, only 45% of the profits of £30,000 is left

Choice 2: Increase salary
Director pays 40% on most of it
Company pays National Insurance contributions at 10.4% on all of it

Pay as salary/bonus

Before	£20,280
Extra	£27,174
After	£47,454

	After
Additional National Insurance	£ 2,826
Additional tax	£ 9,604
Government gets	£12,430
Director gets	£17,570
	£30,000

58.5% of £30,000 left to director after tax and National Insurance

Choice 3: Declare a dividend
Director to get £22,275
Wife to get £225
(after Advance Corporation Tax (ACT) paid by company)
Director pays some tax @ 40%
Wife reclaims tax deducted
(no other income)
Company pays no National Insurance contributions on the dividend

Husband gets	£22,275	
less higher rate tax	£ 3,190	
		£19,085
Wife gets	£ 225	
plus rebate	£ 75	
		£ 300
Total		£19,385

Director (and wife) retain 64.5% of £30,000

Choice 4: Make a pension contribution
No income tax payable
No National Insurance contributions payable
No Corporation Tax (unless spread over)

Company pension contribution	£30,000
Income tax	nil
National Insurance	nil
Corporation Tax	nil
Available for investment	£30,000

100% left after tax

Choice 5: Part salary/part pension
£15,000 paid as extra salary to director, who makes maximum pension contribution out of his total salary
£15,000 paid direct into director's pension scheme

Salary increase	£15,000
less National Insurance	£ 1,413
	£13, 587

Contributes maximum to pension, i.e. 15% of total salary, £33,867 (£20,280 + £13,587)	£5,080
Taxable	£8,507
less: Tax payable	£2,137
Extra 'take-home pay'	£6,370

Director benefits from 88% of the £30,000.

Personal pensions
Why shouldn't executives of small companies be happy with personal pensions? Leaving apart the tax breaks for the company, if you are a young executive there is no reason why a personal pension shouldn't suit you if you keep up your contributions to somewhere near the maximum the Inland Revenue will allow you to pay. If within those figures you get contribution waiver benefit and protection for your dependants against your early death, you should be able to achieve virtual parity with an executive plan with less complications (see Chapter Four for details of contribution limits).

If you are older, and have left pension planning too late in the day and the most that you and/or your company can afford to contribute is within the Inland Revenue contribution limits, then you might as well choose a personal pension. For example, if you are aged fifty-six to sixty, you can contribute up to 35% of your normal earnings, and if you are aged sixty-one or more then you can contribute 40%. You can also pay extra contributions based on your earnings for the previous six years. Roughly, this means that if you are sixty, then you can pay contributions that are equal to some two and a half times your earnings (ignoring any annual increments).

You would need to spread payments over though, because you can't contribute more than your net relevant earnings in any one tax year. And only you, not your employer, can make contributions for previous years.

Final salary schemes

If you are in the final salary scheme of a reasonably large company you may be allowed to build up your pension at up to twice the speed of the normal employee on what is called an 'accelerated accrual rate'. For example, if you are an employee in a company running a final salary scheme based on 60ths (meaning that for every year you are in the scheme you would normally qualify for 1/60th of a year's salary when you retire) you may be allowed to qualify for up to 2/60ths for each year.

This arrangement is very helpful for the executive who joined the company relatively late because it means that they can retire on a full two-thirds pension after only twenty years instead of the usual forty years. So if he joins a company at forty-five he still has time to build up the maximum pension by the state retirement age of sixty-five.

Executives who before 17 March 1987 were in a final salary scheme which allowed accelerated accrual, may be allowed to build up their pension faster than that and get the maximum pension after a mere ten years. But the rules changed in 1987 and no newcomers to final salary schemes are allowed to do this any more. Appendix Two shows the different rates at which you are allowed to accrue benefits.

If even an accelerated accrual rate will not help you to achieve the full two-thirds final pension, then you can consider buying Additional Voluntary Contributions (AVCs) or as long as you are not a 20% director, Freestanding AVCs (FSAVCs). The total contribution an executive can make to all pension arrangements is 15%

of pensionable salary, and the benefits payable may not exceed the limits laid down by the Inland Revenue. There are various ways of building up your fund. The investment options are similar to those available under personal pensions; these are described in Chapter Five.

Inheritance Tax
This chapter would not be complete without a mention of the role to be played by an executive pension plan or SSAS in Inheritance Tax planning, especially for shareholding directors of family companies. If you want to see the next generation carry on the business, an executive pension plan or SSAS should be an integral part of your thinking. Inheritance Tax rules provide great scope for minimising Inheritance Tax by means of gifts. However, if you depend on your capital assets, such as shares in the company, to provide you with your income in later years, then Inheritance Tax saving through outright gifts is impossible. If, on the other hand, you have a secure income independent of capital assets so that you can make outright gifts, then you can save a great deal of tax. Often good pension provision is the foundation of Inheritance Tax planning. You will need to consult your financial adviser on how best to minimise the potential Inheritance Tax bill on your estate.

CHAPTER SEVEN:
MAKING THE BEST OF
YOUR PENSION

There is more to getting the best out of your pension than just swapping your pay packet for a pension cheque. For a start, if you have a personal pension you do not necessarily have to take all the money at once. You might prefer to draw your money in stages, thereby building in some inflation-proofing. Or, if you are going to have some other income, you might not wish to draw your pension for a while. Drawing a pension early will decrease its value and drawing it later should enhance your income.

Questions you need to answer:

- Can you afford to retire early?
- Do you want to retire at the statutory retirement age?
- Do you want to retire late?
- Should you take part of your pension as a lump sum?
- Should you use the fund to take an income for life?
- If you have a personal pension, what sort of annuity should you get?
- Do you want to increase your income or your capital?

Early retirement
Retiring early has become very fashionable; if you have

been careful with your money, have a good pension behind you, or have received a nice inheritance you may wish to do so. On the other hand, you might want to leave your main career behind and set up a small business of your own, secure in the knowledge that you have your pension to fall back on.

Before making the decision to retire early you ought to have a pensions audit (see Chapter One) to make sure that you can afford it. For instance, the mortgage is usually one of the worst expenses; will it be paid off or are your repayments so small that they hardly come into the equation? Will your retirement income be enough to live on happily? Or will you have to scratch around to make ends meet?

— State pensions

As far as the state pensions are concerned, you will not be able to draw either the basic state pension or SERPS until you reach the statutory pensionable age, currently sixty for women and sixty-five for men although both the Labour and Conservative parties have plans to change this. Also, you ought to bear in mind that unless you continue to pay National Insurance contributions at the voluntary rate of £5.05 (1991–92) a week, your basic state pension might be reduced when you draw it. To keep it intact, women normally need to pay National Insurance for about forty years and men for forty-four years. Your pension will be scaled down if you pay for fewer years.

Example:
A man aged fifty-five wants to retire early. He has paid his Class 1 National Insurance contributions since he was twenty-one years old and has thirty-four qualifying years. If he does not continue to pay contributions he will get a pension of 78% of the maximum, currently £40.56 a week, at age sixty-five.

If he decides to pay Class 3 National Insurance until he

is sixty-five he will then get the full pension of £52. In other words he will have to give up about £5 a week for ten years to get £11.50 a week added to his pension for life. As state pensions are increased annually in line with inflation it should more or less hold its buying power, so you should seriously consider paying the voluntary contributions.

Married women who opted to pay at the reduced married women's rate do not qualify for the basic state pension in their own right. However, if they are widowed, they will probably qualify for a pension on the basis of their husband's contributions. If the wife is in SERPS, this too will be reduced as there will be fewer years in which to build it up. Don't forget that the Department of Social Security will give you a forecast of your future basic state pension and SERPS if you get Form BR19. Chapter Two tells you how.

Table L: BASIC PENSION: QUALIFICATIONS

The percentage of the basic state pension you can expect if you retire early, having paid Class 1 National Insurance contributions for enough years so far, and do not elect to pay voluntary contributions of £5.05 a week.

Qualifying years	Men		Women	
	%	£	%	£
44	100	52.00	100	52.00
43	98	50.96	100	52.00
42	96	49.92	100	52.00
41	94	48.88	100	52.00
40	91	47.32	100	52.00
39	89	46.28	98	50.96
38	87	45.24	95	49.40
37	85	44.20	93	48.36
36	82	42.64	90	46.80
35	80	41.60	88	45.76

Source: 'A Guide to Retirement Pensions', Booklet No. NP46, available free from the Department of Social Security. This is a useful guide to state pensions.

— *Occupational pensions*

Most company schemes have traditionally set the same standard retirement ages as the state, i.e. sixty for women and sixty-five for men but this is changing as many are now making the ages equal. While the Inland Revenue will allow men to draw their occupational pension from age fifty and women from age forty-five or ten years before their normal retirement age, whichever is the later, company pension schemes tend to penalise you if you retire early. If you are in a final salary scheme you may qualify for 1/60th pension for every year's service, but you do not usually get that if you retire early. Therefore, by retiring early, you not only lose the opportunity to build up a bigger pension, but also the value of your contributions is likely to be reduced for every such year, which could be very painful. If you wish to retire early you should check the company pension handbook to see whether it will adversely affect your pension.

You should also check what will happen to your pension if you delay drawing it. If you leave your company after 1 January 1991 the worst the company can do is to peg your pension at the date you left and then annually add on 5% or annual increases in the Retail Prices Index (whichever is the lower). The company must then pay this increased figure. The company may increase your pension by a larger figure, even fully inflation-proof it, if it operates a generous scheme. Different rules again will apply if it is contracted-out.

Obviously, if you opt to defer your pension in this way, you will need to make sure that you have enough to live on in the meantime. However, if you retire early on

128

grounds of ill-health you may not suffer financially as well. You could get the full pension you qualified for so far. Much depends on the attitude of your pension scheme trustees who may credit you with the pension you would have earned if you had been able to work to normal retirement age. For example, if you had been in the 1/60th pension scheme for twenty years and would normally expect to put in another ten years before retirement, the trustees may agree to give you a pension assuming thirty years' service – i.e. 30/60ths or half pay.

— Money purchase schemes

If you are contributing to the firm's money purchase pension you should find out the size of your fund before going ahead with your retirement plans. You should ask the personnel department for details and you could also ask them how much income the fund would generate at current interest rates. Basically, they will arrange to buy you the type of annuity you want (see Annuities, page 135). If the scheme is contracted-out, you can't take that part of the benefit until you reach age sixty.

If you have an old-style personal pension (a Section 226 retirement annuity plan) you will not be able to start drawing it until you reach age sixty, but it may be worth your while converting it to a new-style personal pension. Likewise, if you have a Section 32 buy-out plan, you may not be able to start drawing it before the retirement age of the scheme from which the money came, but you can convert it to a new-style personal pension. However, it is worth checking how much the insurance company will penalise you for doing this. You could have another problem with buy-out plans if the company scheme you left was contracted-out of SERPS. Embedded in the plan will be something called a Guaranteed Minimum Pension (GMP). This is the part of the pension that was bought with your National Insurance contributions

129

rebate to the company. You can take the benefits before state pensionable age, as long as the pension paid is at least equal to the Guaranteed Minimum Pension.

The rules are different for personal pensions which you pay for either completely or partly with your National Insurance contributions rebate. If your personal pension is entirely paid for this way, then you will not be able to draw it until state retirement age. If your personal pension is partly paid for out of your rebate, then that part of your fund cannot usually be used until you reach state retirement age.

If you wish to consider retiring early, you should check how much money is in your fund and the prices of annuities that your pension provider offers. At the same time you should ask your financial adviser to find the best rates. The best pension fund investment companies do not necessarily offer the best annuity rates (see Annuities, page 136).

If you have your own personal pension, timing the cashing-in of your fund can be quite critical. If your fund is unit-linked and the stock market is performing badly then it might be a good idea to delay drawing your pension, or to only draw part of it. Conversely, because the income you can get from annuities is influenced by prevailing interest rates and because interest rates tend to be higher when the stock market is down, you might then get a better income at this time. It is all a matter of judgement and your individual requirements.

Retiring at normal age

If you retire with a company pension at the normal age your main consideration is probably whether you should take part of your pension as a tax-free sum (see Commuting your pension, page 133). If you work for a company with a final salary scheme, your decision is final and cannot be changed. This means that once you start drawing your pension you will receive that level of income, plus any inflation-proofing built in until you die.

However, if you wish to retire at the normal age with a personal pension (old-style or new-style) you might like to consider the merits of drawing your pension in stages. The advantage of doing this is that you have the chance to boost your retirement income. For instance, if you draw half, or two-thirds of your pension fund at Stage One of your retirement, then you can leave the rest of your fund to build up until you need to increase your retirement income. By then your fund should have grown and you can start drawing the remaining part of your pension as you wish.

The ability to draw your pension in stages can be quite a useful tool if, for example, you intend to carry on working part-time or if your spouse or partner is able to bring in enough money to pay some of the bills meantime. The longer you leave your pension, the greater its potential size.

Retiring late

Some people will be fortunate enough to actually enjoy their work and not want to be forced to retire just because they have reached state retirement age. Some may be unlucky enough to need to carry on working because their pension planning started too late or because they could not afford to save enough. However, there are some financial rewards for retiring late. For example, the state increases both your basic state pension and SERPS by about 37.5% over the five years after state retirement age. As it is inflation-proofed as well this could be worth the waiting. The choices are fully explained in Chapter Two. It works like this: for every week you delay taking your pension, each £1 of pension will increase by 1/7th of a penny, provided that you do this for at least seven weeks during the five years starting on the day you reached state pensionable age.

An easier figure to remember is that it increases by about 7.5% each year. At today's prices, with the full basic state pension at £52 a week (£2,704 p.a.) your pension will increase to about £55.90 (£2,906.80 p.a.), if you defer it for one year and to £71.50 a week (£3,718 p.a.) if you defer it for the full five years. In the case of a married couple, who currently would get £83.25 a week (£4,329 p.a.) between them, it would rise to about £89.49 a week (£4,653 p.a.) at the end of the first year and then to £114.46 a week (£5,925 p.a.) at the end of five years. SERPS and the Graduated Pension (for what that's worth) will go up by the same percentage. You have to defer all your state pensions together, you cannot defer just one of them.

The state system is quite flexible. If you opt to defer your state pension, you can change your mind at any time. It makes sense to choose the end of a seven-week period, counting from the day you reached state pensionable age, as payments will not be made for part of seven weeks. Also, once you have started drawing the state pension, you can stop at any time within five years and start building up an increased pension for later. However, you can only change your mind once. You cannot get any more increases after you are sixty-five (women) or seventy (men).

Do remember to tell the Department of Social Security of your plans. They should write to you four months before you reach the statutory retirement age 'inviting' you to claim your pension. Also, if you have started drawing your pension and want to stop, you need to inform them. Just stopping cashing your pension is not sufficient. You should complete Department of Social Security Form BR 432 in DSS leaflet N192, 'Giving Up Your Retirement Pension to Earn Extra'.

If you defer your state pension for the full five years

you will need to live for another thirteen and a half years to break even and get the maximum benefit in terms of the money you have not drawn. This means that men will have to live until they are about eighty-three and women until they are seventy-eight to benefit. These figures exceed the normal life expectancy of men, but not of women and, therefore, there is more advantage for women to defer their state pensions for the full five years than for men. Figures from the Government Actuary's Department show that women can expect to live until age eighty-one, while men retiring can expect to live to age seventy-eight.

Just because you are not drawing your state pension does not mean that you cannot draw your personal pension or your occupational pension. On the other hand, you can draw the state pension and leave your other pensions to build up. Alternatively, you can draw your state pensions and invest the money in a personal pension for future use providing you are still earning. In order to pay all your basic state pension of £52 a week (£2,704 p.a.) into a personal pension you will need to be earning £7,725 a year if you are a woman aged sixty, or £6,760 if you are aged sixty-one plus; if you are a man aged sixty-five you will need minimum earnings of £6,760 p. a. This calculation does not include SERPS because the figures vary so much between different people. It is based on the fact that the Inland Revenue allows people aged fifty-six to sixty to contribute 35% of their earnings into a personal pension and people aged sixty-one and more to contribute 40%.

Should you take a lump sum?
Most pension schemes allow you to draw off a lump sum when you retire. You can usually do this by sacrificing some of your potential retirement income. Employees in the public sector however, usually get a pension that is

based on 80ths plus a lump sum. Most other people have to make the decision for themselves.

The maximum lump sum you can draw from a final salary scheme is one and a half times your final salary. Employees who joined a pension scheme after 14 March 1989 suffer an 'earnings cap' which means that earnings over £71,400 p.a. don't count. If your final salary is £20,000 the maximum lump sum you can draw is £30,000. In practice few people ever qualify for a full pension or lump sum. What usually happens is that the maximum lump sum you can draw is 3/80ths of final salary for every year you have been in the scheme. So if you have been in the firm's final salary scheme for twenty years, the maximum lump sum you can get is 3/80ths final salary × 20, i.e. 60/80ths or three-quarters of your pay.

However, if you take the cash your pension income will suffer. The amount by which it will be reduced depends on your age and sex, but in broad terms you can expect your pension to be reduced by about £1 for each £10 of cash you take.

The actual recommended reduction is on a straightforward sliding scale of between 8.19% for women aged fifty-five and 10.2% for women aged sixty-five; 9.8% for men aged sixty and 12.8% for men aged seventy. Therefore, the longer you wait to draw your pension the less it is reduced for the same amount of lump sum.

Usually, the maximum you can take as a lump sum if you have a money purchase scheme, whether an occupational scheme or a personal pension, is 25% of the fund. However, if the scheme has contracted-out of SERPS, the part of the fund that was paid for with the National Insurance rebate cannot be swapped or used when working out the size of the fund for this purpose.

Whether you opt for a lump sum or not depends mainly on whether you want to maximise your income which is, after all, what pensions are all about. Purists argue that you should take all the fund as income because it is deferred pay. However, if you belong to a company pension scheme which does not offer a fully inflation-proofed pension, you might well do better by drawing the biggest lump sum you can and buying an inflation-proofed purchased life annuity with it to supplement your main pension. Likewise, if you have a personal pension you might like to buy a level annuity with 75% of the fund, and a purchased life annuity with the 25% lump sum you draw off (see Table M, page 140).

Annuities

First we will look at annuities and the choices you have. Picking a good pension fund is a piece of cake compared with the complications of choosing an annuity. Very little is published about them and yet they are one of the most crucial financial planning decisions you can make.

A pension annuity provides an income for life. It is bought with your pension fund from the cash available after taking out any lump sum you wish to draw. You have no option but to buy an annuity, also called a compulsory purchase annuity (CPA) with your pension fund, apart from any lump sum you draw. The government has allowed you handsome tax relief on your contributions to encourage you to be independent in your retirement and not be a burden on the state, and they will not allow you to renege on the contract once you retire. In a way, buying an annuity is rather like investing a lump sum in a high interest building society account – the main difference being that you cannot get your capital back from an annuity. However, in exchange you should get a better guaranteed return for your money than you would by investing it for income anywhere else. You are guaranteed an income for life regardless of how long you live, whether for ten years or fifty years. It's the guarantee that sets it apart.

Suppose you buy a simple level 10% annuity with a pension fund of £100,000. The insurance company will pay you £10,000 a year for the rest of your life. Basically, that means that you get your capital back in ten years, but they carry on paying you £10,000 a year for as long as you live, regardless of what happens to interest rates anywhere else. This is unlike a building society high interest account where the income will fluctuate in line with interest rates.

Most people tend to buy their annuity from the insurance company with which they have built up their pension fund. This can be a most expensive mistake as you may get a higher level of income elsewhere. You have what is called an 'open market option' to buy your annuity from any authorised insurance company. The company that holds your funds may penalise you for taking the money away from them, but that can be a small price to pay for an improved annuity. Recent surveys show a 20% difference in the return offered from the best and the worst. So it really pays to ask your financial adviser to find the best deal for you. In a way it's rather like shopping around for the best building society high interest account.

There are various types of annuities, each offering a different rate of return. The rates vary according to factors such as:

● Your age when you take it out
● Your sex
● Whether you want to be paid monthly in advance or arrears, quarterly or annually
● Whether you want a level payment annuity, one which pays out the same sum for life, or whether you want to build in some increases to offset the effect of inflation
● Whether you want a with-profits plan, or unit-linked

plan which is designed to increase your income in line with the fortunes of the Stock Exchange

● Whether you want the guarantees to be for five or ten years

● Whether you want an annuity to be paid to your spouse if you die before them

— Age

The older you are when you buy an annuity, the higher your income will be. Obviously the actuaries do not expect a seventy-year-old to live as long as a sixty-year-old and therefore will be more generous. Even a couple of years can make quite a significant difference in the payments.

— Gender

Men get significantly bigger annuities than women of the same age because statistically they are expected to live for a shorter time. So the insurance company does not expect to have to pay out for as long as in the case of their female counterparts.

— Payment intervals

Most people will expect to receive their pension cheque monthly, but if you are paid monthly in arrears you can increase your income a little. You can boost it further if it is paid quarterly in arrears. This is partly because the insurance company holds on to the money for longer and partly because there is reduced administration. Whether you make the decision to receive your cheque a quarter or a year in arrears will depend on your financial circumstances.

— Level payments

These are the simplest option. They are usually the most popular as initially you get the biggest possible pension but their real value will decrease as inflation erodes their buying power. If inflation runs at 7.5% the pension will halve in value over ten years and will reduce to one-third in fifteen years. If you are going to rely entirely on an annuity for future income and expect to be drawing it for many years then you should consider annuities which pay out an increasing income.

— Increasing payments
By sacrificing some income in the early days you can have an increasing pension. You may have the choice of levels of increase: normally 3%, 5%, 8.5% or Retail Prices Index. Whichever level you choose you will then get a pension that rises at the specified rate for the rest of your life.

You may be able partially to inflation-proof your income by buying a with-profits plan or unit-linked plan. In a with-profits annuity you can expect annual bonuses which should increase your income over the distance. Unit-linked annuities are more risky and not for the timid. As unit-linked funds tend to be more volatile, the value of your fund can go down as well as up. What happens is that your payments are calculated on a pre-determined number of units which are cashed for you every time they make a payment. If the value of the units is low, then your income will reduce, likewise if the value increases then your pension will increase. This means that your income will fluctuate, sometimes substantially, which is disconcerting and rarely appropriate for a pension.

— Five and ten year guarantees
Many people are worried about what will happen to their fund if they die shortly after starting to draw their pension. They think it is unfair to have built up a good pension and then find their family loses the benefit if

they die early. You can get around this by accepting a reduced pension and buying a guaranteed annuity. Most people want a five-year guarantee but some prefer a ten-year guarantee. This usually means that if you die within five years (or ten years) of drawing your pension the company continues to pay the income to your estate until the agreed period has elapsed. Payments are made at the same rate as if you were alive, or sometimes they can be paid in one lump sum.

— Spouse's pension
Some people want to leave their spouse with a pension if they die before their partner. Again, at the expense of some current income, you can arrange for this facility. The amount by which the pension will be reduced will depend on the age and sex of your spouse. Therefore, a man with a very young wife will lose more than a woman with an older husband. Obviously the insurance companies will not want to have to pay a forty-year-old widow a pension until she dies without charging significantly for this.

Purchased Life Annuities
The type of annuity you choose will depend on your financial circumstances, responsibilities to any dependants and your attitude to risk.

While you have to buy a pensions annuity with the bulk of your fund, you can gain some tax benefits by buying a purchased life annuity with the lump sum. This makes sense if your main priority is to increase your income. You can make gains by buying a purchased life annuity because the Inland Revenue accepts that part of your income is a return of capital which is not taxable. The following table shows how it works:

Table M: ANNUITIES

The difference in income between:

a) buying a pension annuity with the lot – £100,000
b) buying a purchased life annuity with a lump sum from a personal pension fund of £100,000, plus a pension annuity with the remaining £75,000;

Annuity rate: pension annuity 7.14%; life annuity 7.16%
Male sixty-five, paying basic rate tax at 25%

	(a) Pension annuity only	(b) Pension annuity plus life annuity
Income each year	£7,141	£5,355
Taxable income from life annuity	nil	£1,152
Sub total	£7,141	£6,507
Less tax @ 25%	£1,786	£1,626
Net annual income	£5,355	£4,880
Plus return of capital	nil	£ 517
Total income	£5,355	£5,397

Tax saved is £160, and income is increased by £42.

Income boosters

There are various ways to invest your lump sum for income. If you do not wish to take any risks then you can choose between:

● High interest deposit accounts from banks or building societies which pay monthly income
● National Savings Income Bonds and Tax Exempt Special Savings Accounts (TESSAs) which are similar to high interest accounts except that the interest is tax free. For TESSAs the money has to remain invested for

five years. If you are prepared to take some risk you should consider alternatives, such as investment bonds and income personal equity plans

— *Deposit accounts*

High interest deposit accounts are mainly available from building societies and banks. Many of them now offer you the facility to draw the interest monthly or half-yearly, rather than waiting for the full year. If you draw the interest you keep your capital intact, but it will never have the opportunity to grow. However, if income is a priority, these accounts have the advantage of security and accessibility. The main disadvantage is that the real spending power of your capital will decrease as inflation rises.

– *National Savings Income Bonds*

National Savings Income Bonds are absolutely safe and the interest is paid with no tax deducted which makes them ideal for non-taxpayers as they do not need to go to the bother of retrospectively reclaiming the tax paid. They are also good value for tax-payers who have to declare the interest only once a year. The bonds cost £1,000 each and you have to buy at least two. The maximum holding is £25,000. They pay an income of 11.75% (20 June 1991).

How much will your income be?

Holding	Monthly income (average*)	Annual income at 11.75%
£ 2,000	£ 19.58	£ 235.50
£ 5,000	£ 48.95	£ 587.50
£10,000	£ 97.90	£1,175.00
£25,000	£244.79	£2,937.50

* The precise amount payable varies dependent upon the number of days in each month.

— *Investment Bonds*

Investment bonds are a simple way of investing a lump sum either for growth or income but they are especially useful for producing tax-free 'income'. They are a pooled investment in which you get a specified number of units for your money. There is usually a higher minimum investment, often £5,000, than for unit trusts which they resemble.

The money is normally invested in equities and you can usually choose from a range of funds with free switching options. As these are equity-based investments, there is a risk that your money will go down as well as up but they are generally considered to be less volatile than managed unit trusts.

You can get tax-free 'income' by cashing in up to 5% of your initial investment each year for twenty years, while leaving the rest, hopefully, to grow. If you do not draw cash in any year you can carry that year's 5% to the next year. Likewise, if you do not draw anything for the first two years you can draw 15% in the third year. If you do not draw anything for twenty years you can withdraw the whole of your initial investment free of tax, but you may be liable to higher rate tax on any profits. This income facility is especially useful for higher rate taxpayers.

You can arrange to draw more than 5% a year. In many cases this will be tax free for basic rate taxpayers, but any income you draw in excess of 5% must be added to your other income. If that takes you into the higher rate tax bracket you will have to pay tax on the difference between the basic rate and the higher rate, i.e. 40% − 25% = 15% on the amount of the withdrawal above 5%.

Example:
Herbert Nicholas is a higher rate taxpayer who wants to draw £75 a month (9% p.a.) from a £10,000 bond:

Total income (12 × £75)	£900
Less 5% allowance (5% × £10,000)	£500
Excess	£400

Tax payable: 15% × £400 = £60
Total income: £900 − £60 = £840

— *TESSAs*

TESSAs are designed as five-year savings plans but you can draw tax-free income from them provided you stick to the rules. They were first available on 1 January 1991 and you can invest up to £3,000 in year one (£6,000 for a couple) in a TESSA and up to £9,000 in total over five years.

— *Income PEPs*

Income Personal Equity Plans (PEPs) can produce some healthy income at the same time as having the potential to increase in value. As a PEP is an equity-linked investment its value can go down as well as up, so you should consult your financial adviser about suitable plans and the level of risk you are prepared to accept. However, it could be worth putting some of your lump sum into this type of investment.

Sample income portfolio:
Husband and wife with £50,000 lump sum could consider the following investments:
£ 3,000 each in a TESSA (total £6,000)
£10,000 National Savings Income Bond in wife's name
£ 9,000 high income savings account, bank or building society, in joint names
£10,000 one-year guaranteed income bond in husband's name
£ 6,000 each in an investment bond (total £12,000)
£ 3,000 in income unit trusts in wife's name

You should check out whether this sort of portfolio will be suitable for you. A lot depends on how old you are, what tax you already pay and what other investments you hold, to name but three considerations to be taken into account.

Growth boosters
If you wish to invest your capital for growth, you should consider how accessible and safe you want it to be. There are four categories of investment opportunities for you:

- Savings on short call, i.e. instant access building society or bank high interest accounts. These accounts are partly intended to cushion you from emergencies such as the roof falling in, or a sudden family disaster where someone needs cash urgently, and partly to give you an instant source of cash in case an irresistible investment opportunity turns up
- Completely safe investments which may offer a better rate of return than building societies, for example gilt-edged securities
- Medium risk investments such as ten-year with-profits endowment policies which lock in gains made each year but where the return is still uncertain since it is linked to stock market performance
- Higher risk investments in carefully selected investment bonds, unit trusts, investment trusts and unit-linked life policies

Spreading your lump sum between these various options is very much a matter of personal preference. It will depend on your attitude to risk in general, your view of the potential returns of an investment and your financial circumstances. Overall, it would probably be wise to keep a sum equal to between three and six months' required income on short call and divide the rest between the others.

Sample capital growth portfolio:
A husband and wife with a £50,000 lump sum
No risk:
£5,000 each in National Savings, index-linked (total £10,000)
£3,000 each in a TESSA (total £6,000)
£9,000 National Savings Income Bond in wife's name
Medium risk:
£5,000 each in an investment bond (total £10,000)
£6,000 each in a PEP (total £12,000)
£3,000 unit trust in wife's name

Remember that these are only ideas. You should think carefully about the right portfolio for you.

APPENDIX ONE:
DSS PENSION FORECAST

Department of Social Security
Central Office Room 37D Longbenton
Newcastle-upon-Tyne NE98 1YX

MRS. A A
1
1

Your reference number is

AA111111A/PAB/7

Please tell your local Social Security Office
this number if you contact them in writing
or by phone

Date: **16 July 1991**

YOUR PENSION FORECAST

DEAR MRS A,

This letter is the Retirement Pension Forecast that you
asked us to send you.

The Total Retirement Pension you may be entitled to
According to our information and our calculations:

– if you were getting a State Retirement Pension now,
you would be entitled to £41.03 a week based on our
present National Insurance contribution records.

- by the time you are 60, assuming your earnings go up at the same rate as prices, you are likely to be entitled to a State Retirement Pension that would be £59.29 a week if you were getting it now. If your earnings go up at 1.5% above the rate that prices are going up, you are likely to be entitled to a State Retirement Pension that would be £59.72 a week if you were getting it now.

The information in this Forecast is based on:

- the rules about Retirement Pension that apply at the moment.
- the National Insurance (NI) contributions that you already have, and that we think you will have using the information you gave us on your application form, by the time you are 60.
- the Retirement Pension rates for this year. We cannot tell you how much the rates will be when you start getting your Retirement Pension because they normally go up every April, to keep up with rises in prices. So the amounts in this letter are the amounts you would get if you were getting your Retirement Pension now.

The Forecast is right if:

- your date of birth is 7 July 1941.
- you go on working and paying enough full-rate NI contributions until you are 60.
- the other information you gave us in the application form is right.

The different parts of Retirement Pension
There are a number of different parts of Retirement Pension:

- Basic Pension, based on full-rate NI contributions.
- Additional Pension, based on full-rate NI contributions paid on earnings since 6 April 1978.
- Graduated Retirement Benefit, based on any graduated contributions you paid between 6 April 1961 and 5 April 1975.

We explain in this letter how much you may be entitled to for each part.

Basic Pension
To get Basic Pension you need to have enough National Insurance (NI) contributions in enough years. The rules about what count as enough NI contributions and enough years are quite complicated. If you want to know more, detailed information about this is in NP46 ("A Guide to State Retirement Pensions").

Our records, up to 5 April 1991, show that you do not have enough NI contributions to get the full amount of Basic Pension. You only have enough to get 37% of the full amount. This would be £19.24 a week if you were getting Basic Pension now.

If you go on working and pay enough full-rate NI contributions for the 10 tax years between 6 April 1991 and 5 April 2001 you could get 64% of the full amount. This would be £33.28 a week if you were getting Basic Pension now.

Basic Pension for married women
As you are a married woman, you may be able to get more Basic Pension by using your husband's National Insurance (NI) contributions. What you would receive and when depends on the dates you and your husband reach State pension age and claim your State Retirement Pensions. But you could get up to 60% of the full amount. This would be £31.25 a week if you were getting it now.

To get Basic Pension using your husband's NI contributions:

- he must be age 65 or over and getting a Basic Pension, and
- you must be age 60 or over and made a proper claim to State Retirement Pension.

But please remember, the total Basic Pension using your husband's NI contributions cannot be more than 60% of the full amount. And it would include any Basic Pension you were already entitled to using your own NI contributions.

If you want to know more, detailed information about this is in NP46 ("A Guide to State Retirement Pensions").

Home Responsibilities Protection (HRP)

Certain people who stay at home to look after someone can have their Basic Pension safeguarded even though they do not pay full-rate NI contributions. The Law helps to protect the Basic Pension rights of these people if they have had home responsibilities at any time since 6th April 1978. So, as long as they are not women who have kept the right to pay reduced-rate NI contributions in that tax year, they can get HRP for each full tax year after 6 April 1978 when:

- they get Child Benefit as the main payee for a child under age 16, or
- they look after someone getting Attendance or Constant Attendance Allowance for at least 35 hours a week, or
- they get Income Support so that they can stay off work to look after an elderly or sick person at home, or
- they have a mixture of any of these home responsibilities.

These rules also apply to people who are working but do not pay enough full-rate NI contributions for them to count towards Retirement Pension.

But please remember:

- paying enough full-rate NI contributions in a tax year can sometimes give a higher amount of Basic Pension than a tax year of HRP.
- certain people can get Invalid Care Allowance if they are looking after someone getting Attendance or Constant Attendance Allowance. They can then be "credited" with a NI contribution for each week that Invalid Care Allowance is payable, so they may not have to depend on HRP or pay voluntary (Class 3) NI contributions.

If you want to know more, detailed information is in Leaflet NP27 ("Looking after someone at home? How to protect your pension").

Our records show that up to and including 5 April 1991, you may be entitled to 3 years of HRP. If you think you are entitled to more HRP up to that date, please take this letter to your local Social Security office. When we worked out your Forecast we did not count any years of HRP that you may get in the future.

National Insurance (NI) contributions – some general information
Women who are working and already paying NI contributions will still have to pay these contributions if they go on working until they are 60.

Paying NI contributions not paid in the past – the effect on your Basic Pension
Certain people who have not paid enough NI contributions in the past can sometimes get more Basic Pension

by paying voluntary (Class 3) NI contributions. These can be paid when there is no requirement to pay Class 1 contributions as an employee or Class 2 contributions as a self-employed person. The rules about the payment of these contributions are quite complicated so if you want to know more, detailed information is in Leaflet NI42 and Leaflet NI48.

Our records show that you have enough NI contributions and credits in the time limits allowed up to 5 April 1991 to count towards your Basic Pension, so you cannot improve your Basic Pension by paying any other NI contributions you may not have paid in the past. This is because:

- you cannot pay NI contributions if they are for a period before you joined the National Insurance scheme.
- you cannot pay NI contributions if they are for a period more than 6 years before the end of the last full tax year (a tax year always starts on the 6th April and ends on the 5th April).

Additional Pension: what this is
Additional Pension is the part of your Retirement Pension that is based on any full-rate NI contributions you paid as an employee on earnings since 6 April 1978. It is sometimes called SERPS – the State Earnings-Related Pension Scheme.

We have worked out your Additional Pension based on the latest NI contribution records that we hold for you. It may not include the value of all the contributions you may have paid in either the present or previous tax year, but we tell you in the next main paragraph the latest tax year on which your Additional Pension has been worked out.

If you are, or have ever been, a member of a contracted-out occupational pension scheme used instead of SERPS

151

and have built up rights to a pension from such a scheme, a reduction will be made to your Additional Pension. This reduction is known as a Contracted-out Deduction. The same applies if you are, or have ever been, a member of a personal pension scheme used instead of SERPS.

Please remember, the amount of any Additional Pension you get from the State may be different if in the future you decide to leave or join a contracted-out occupational pension scheme used instead of SERPS. The same applies if you ever leave or join a personal pension scheme used instead of SERPS.

If you want to know more about Additional Pension, detailed information is in NP46 ("A Guide to State Retirement Pensions").

Additional Pension: what you are already entitled to
Our records up to 5 April 1991 show that you are already entitled to an Additional Pension of £19.75 a week payable by the State. This is how we worked it out:

Total Additional Pension	£26.02
less Contracted-out Deduction of	£ 6.27
Additional Pension payable by the State	£19.75

Additional Pension: what you will be entitled to when you are 60
If you go on working until you are 60 you will be entitled to a bigger Additional Pension. We have worked out how much you would get, as if you had already worked until you were 60 and were getting your Additional Pension now.

We have worked this out in two ways, using your highest earnings in the last 5 years when you paid contributions:

1. As if each year until you are 60 your earnings go up at the same rate as prices are going up at the moment.

Working it out this way you will get an Additional Pension of £23.97 a week payable by the State. This is how we worked it out:

Total Additional Pension	£51.32
less Contracted-out Deduction of	£27.35
Additional Pension payable by the State	£23.97

2. As if each year until you are 60 your earnings go up at 1.5% more than the rate that prices are going up at the moment.

Working it out this way you will get an Additional Pension of £24.40 a week payable by the State. This is how we worked it out:

Total Additional Pension	£53.92
less Contracted-out Deduction of	£29.52
Additional Pension payable by the State	£24.40

Graduated Retirement Benefit (GRB)

Our records show that you have 30 GRB units from the graduated contributions that you paid between 6 April 1961 and 5 April 1975. At the moment your total GRB entitlement would be £2.04 a week if you were getting it now. GRB usually goes up each year to keep up with rises in prices.

Extra information

You asked us other questions about your Retirement Pension. We tell you below what will happen if:

153

– you stop working before you are 60:
If you stop working on 7 July 1996 then

- if your earnings go up at the same rate as prices, you are likely to be entitled to a State Retirement Pension that would be £51.88 a week if you were getting it now.
- if your earnings go up at 1.5% more than prices, you are likely to be entitled to a State Retirement Pension that would be £52.04 if you were getting it now.

These amounts are different because your Retirement Pension will change as follows:

- Basic Pension: If we assume that you pay enough full-rate NI contributions or are credited with enough in 6 tax years between 6 April 1991 and 5 April 1997, you could get 53% of the full amount. This would be £27.56 a week if you were getting Basic Pension now.
- Additional Pension: if your earnings go up at the same rate as prices until you stop work you would get an Additional Pension of £22.28 a week payable by the State. This is how we worked it out:

Total Additional Pension	£41.20
less Contracted-out Deduction of	£18.92
Additional Pension payable by the State	£22.28

If your earnings go up at 1.5% more than the rate of prices you would get a total Additional Pension of £22.44 a week payable by the State. This is how we worked it out:

Total Additional Pension	£42.17
less Contracted-out Deduction of	£19.73
Additional Pension payable by the State	£22.44

154

- Graduated Retirement Benefit: this will stay the same at £2.04 a week if you were getting it now.

Please remember, in addition to what we have told you above, if you also pay enough voluntary contributions or are credited with enough for the 4 tax years after the end of the tax year in which you stop working, until you are 60, you could still get 64% of the full rate. This would be £33.28 if you were getting Basic Pension now.

Finally . . .
This letter gives you a lot of information about your Retirement Pension. But it cannot tell you everything you may want to know. This is why we tell you what leaflets to get if you want more detailed information. You can get these leaflets free of charge from any Social Security office. Or you can write for them to the following address, telling them the leaflet titles and reference numbers of the ones you want:

ISCO5 (DSS),
The Paddock,
Frizinghall,
Bradford,
Yorkshire
BD9 4HD

And please remember:

- this is your own Retirement Pension Forecast. It does not include any Retirement Pension that your husband may be entitled to.
- a form inviting you to claim your State Retirement Pension will be sent to you automatically four months before you reach 60. So it is very important that you tell your local Social Security office if you change the

address you gave us on your Forecast application form. But if for some reason you do not get a claim form before you are 60, please go to your local Social Security office without delay for advice.

— you cannot start getting Retirement Pension until you are 60, and have made a proper claim. And remember, you can still get Retirement Pension even if you go on working after you are 60.

— your Forecast has been worked out assuming that the information you gave us on your application form will not change. So if any of the information does change, or the rules about Retirement Pension are altered, then your future entitlement may be different.

— you should keep this letter in a safe place, together with any other information you may get from the Department of Social Security. This is in case you have any queries when you eventually claim your State Retirement Pension.

If you need any more help or advice about your Retirement Pension Forecast, please take this letter NOW to your local Social Security office. The address is in the 'phone book under "Social Security" or "Health and Social Security". Or, if you would rather contact them in writing or by 'phone, please tell them the reference number shown at the top of this letter.

Yours sincerely,

Department of Social Security
Central Office Room 37D Longbenton
Newcastle-upon-Tyne NE98 1YX

MR. A A
1
1

Your reference number is

AA111111A/PAB/7

Please tell your local Social Security Office
this number if you contact them in writing
or by phone

Date: **16 July 1991**

YOUR PENSION FORECAST

DEAR MR A,

This letter is the Retirement Pension Forecast that you
asked us to send you.

The Total Retirement Pension you may be entitled to
According to our information and our calculations:

- if you were getting a State Retirement Pension now,
  you would be entitled to £64.22 a week based on our
  present National Insurance contribution records.
- by the time you are 65, assuming your earnings go up
  at the same rate as prices, you are likely to be entitled
  to a State Retirement Pension that would be £77.61 a
  week if you were getting it now. If your earnings go up
  at 1.5% above the rate that prices are going up, you are
  likely to be entitled to a State Retirement Pension that
  would be £77.91 a week if you were getting it now.

The information in this Forecast is based on:

- the rules about Retirement Pension that apply at the moment.
- the National Insurance (NI) contributions that you already have, and that we think you will have using the information you gave us on your application form, by the time you are 65.
- the Retirement Pension rates for this year. We cannot tell you how much the rates will be when you start getting your Retirement Pension because they normally go up every April, to keep up with rises in prices. So the amounts in this letter are the amounts you would get if you were getting your Retirement Pension now.

The Forecast is right if:

- your date of birth is 7 July 1941.
- you go on working and paying enough full-rate NI contributions until you are 65.
- the other information you gave us in the application form is right.

The different parts of Retirement Pension
There are a number of different parts of Retirement Pension:

- Basic Pension, based on full-rate NI contributions.
- Additional Pension, based on full-rate NI contributions paid on earnings since 6 April 1978.
- Graduated Retirement Benefit, based on any graduated contributions you paid between 6 April 1961 and 5 April 1975.

We explain in this letter how much you may be entitled to for each part.

Basic Pension

To get Basic Pension you need to have enough National Insurance (NI) contributions in enough years. The rules about what count as enough NI contributions and enough years are quite complicated. If you want to know more, detailed information about this is in NP46 ("A Guide to State Retirement Pensions").

Our records, up to 5 April 1991, show that you do not have enough NI contributions to get the full amount of Basic Pension. You only have enough to get 78% of the full amount. This would be £40.56 a week if you were getting Basic Pension now.

If you go on working and pay enough full-rate NI contributions for the 15 tax years between 6 April 1991 and 5 April 2006 you could get the full amount. This would be £52.00 a week if you were getting Basic Pension now. But please remember, this does not take into account any automatic credits that you may become entitled to. We tell you more about these credits later in this letter.

Home Responsibilities Protection (HRP)

Certain people who stay at home to look after someone can have their Basic Pension safeguarded even though they do not pay full-rate NI contributions. The Law helps to protect the Basic Pension rights of these people if they have had home responsibilities at any time since 6th April 1978. So, as long as they are not women who have kept the right to pay reduced-rate NI contributions in that tax year, they can get HRP for each full tax year after 6 April 1978 when:

- they get Child Benefit as the main payee for a child under age 16, or
- they look after someone getting Attendance or Constant Attendance Allowance for at least 35 hours a week, or

- they get Income Support so that they can stay off work to look after an elderly or sick person at home, or
- they have a mixture of any of these home responsibilities.

These rules also apply to people who are working but do not pay enough full-rate NI contributions for them to count towards Retirement Pension.
But please remember:

- paying enough full-rate NI contributions in a tax year can sometimes give a higher amount of Basic Pension than a tax year of HRP.
- certain people can get Invalid Care Allowance if they are looking after someone getting Attendance or Constant Attendance Allowance. They can then be "credited" with a NI contribution for each week that Invalid Care Allowance is payable, so they may not have to depend on HRP or pay voluntary (Class 3) NI contributions.

If you want to know more, detailed information is in Leaflet NP27 ("Looking after someone at home? How to protect your pension").
Our records show that up to and including 5 April 1991, you are not entitled to HRP. If you think you are entitled, please take this letter to your local Social Security office. When we worked out your Forecast we did not count any years of HRP that you may get in the future.

National Insurance (NI) contributions – some general information
Men who are working and already paying NI contributions will still have to pay these contributions if they go on working until they are 65.

Automatic credits for men

A man can get credits instead of having to pay NI contributions for 5 full tax years starting with the one in which he is 60. He can get these credits for each full tax year when:

– he does not work, or
– he works but does not have to pay any NI contributions because his earnings are very low.

We give these credits automatically at the end of each tax year. But he will not get credits for any tax year in which he spends more than 182 days abroad. So if a man has to stop work before he reaches age 65 he can get automatic credits, as long as he does not spend more than 182 days abroad in any one tax year.

NP46 ("A Guide to State Retirement Pensions") gives more information about credits, but if you need help, please ask at your local Social Security office.

Paying NI contributions not paid in the past – the effect on your Basic Pension

Certain people who have not paid enough NI contributions in the past can sometimes get more Basic Pension by paying voluntary (Class 3) NI contributions. These can be paid when there is no requirement to pay Class 1 contributions as an employee or Class 2 contributions as a self-employed person. The rules about the payment of these contributions are quite complicated so if you want to know more, detailed information is in Leaflet NI42 and Leaflet NI48.

Our records show that you have enough NI contributions and credits in the time limits allowed up to 5 April 1991 to count towards your Basic Pension, so you cannot improve your Basic Pension by paying any other

NI contributions you may not have paid in the past. This is because:

- you cannot pay NI contributions if they are for a period before you joined the National Insurance scheme.
- you cannot pay NI contributions if they are for a period more than 6 years before the end of the last full tax year (a tax year always starts on the 6th April and ends on the 5th April).

Additional Pension: what this is

Additional Pension is the part of your Retirement Pension that is based on any full-rate NI contributions you paid as an employee on earnings since 6 April 1978. It is sometimes called SERPS – the State Earnings-Related Pension Scheme.

We have worked out your Additional Pension based on the latest NI contribution records that we hold for you. It may not include the value of all the contributions you may have paid in either the present or previous tax year, but we tell you in the next main paragraph the latest tax year on which your Additional Pension has been worked out.

If you are, or have ever been, a member of a contracted-out occupational pension scheme used instead of SERPS and have built up rights to a pension from such a scheme, a reduction will be made to your Additional Pension. This reduction is known as a Contracted-out Deduction. The same applies if you are, or have ever been, a member of a personal pension scheme used instead of SERPS.

Please remember, the amount of any Additional Pension you get from the State may be different if in the future you decide to leave or join a contracted-out occupational pension scheme used instead of SERPS. The same applies if you ever leave or join a personal pension scheme used instead of SERPS.

If you want to know more about Additional Pension, detailed information is in NP46 ("A Guide to State Retirement Pensions").

Additional Pension: what you are already entitled to
Our records up to 5 April 1991 show that you are already entitled to an Additional Pension of £21.62 a week payable by the State. This is how we worked it out:

Total Additional Pension	£26.77
less Contracted-out Deduction of	£ 5.15
Additional Pension payable by the State	£21.62

Additional Pension: what you will be entitled to when you are 65
If you go on working until you are 65 you will be entitled to a bigger Additional Pension. We have worked out how much you would get, as if you had already worked until you were 65 and were getting your Additional Pension now.

We have worked this out in two ways, using your highest earnings in the last 5 years when you paid contributions:

1. As if each year until you are 65 your earnings go up at the same rate as prices are going up at the moment.

Working it out this way you will get an Additional Pension of £23.57 a week payable by the State. This is how we worked it out:

Total Additional Pension	£54.70
less Contracted-out Deduction of	£31.13
Additional Pension payable by the State	£23.57

2. As if each year until you are 65 your earnings go up at 1.5% more than the rate that prices are going up at the moment.

Working it out this way you will get an Additional Pension of £23.87 a week payable by the State. This is how we worked it out:

Total Additional Pension	£58.95
less Contracted-out Deduction of	£35.08
Additional Pension payable by the State	£23.87

Graduated Retirement Benefit (GRB)

Our records show that you have 30 GRB units from the graduated contributions that you paid between 6 April 1961 and 5 April 1975. At the moment your total GRB entitlement would be £2.04 a week if you were getting it now. GRB usually goes up each year to keep up with rises in prices.

Extra information

You asked us other questions about your Retirement Pension. We tell you below what will happen if:

– **you stop working before you are 65:**
If you stop working on 7 July 2001 then

– if your earnings go up at the same rate as prices, you are likely to be entitled to a State Retirement Pension that would be £77.09 a week if you were getting it now.
– if your earnings go up at 1.5% more than prices, you are likely to be entitled to a State Retirement Pension that would be £77.25 if you were getting it now.

These amounts are different because your Retirement Pension will change as follows:

– Basic Pension: the amount you could get when you are 65 will stay the same at £52.00 if you were getting it now. This is because you will get automatic credits from when you plan to stop work until you are 65. But if you plan to go abroad for more than 182 days in any of those years you will not get these "credits" and your entitlement may be different.

– Additional Pension: if your earnings go up at the same rate as prices until you stop work you would get an Additional Pension of £23.05 a week payable by the State. This is how we worked it out:

Total Additional Pension	£47.25
less Contracted-out Deduction of	£24.20
Additional Pension payable by the State	£23.05

If your earnings go up at 1.5% more than the rate of prices you would get a total Additional Pension of £23.21 a week payable by the State. This is how we worked it out:

Total Additional Pension	£49.56
less Contracted-out Deduction of	£26.35
Additional Pension payable by the State	£23.21

– Graduated Retirement Benefit: this will stay the same at £2.04 a week if you were getting it now.

Finally . . .
This letter gives you a lot of information about your Retirement Pension. But it cannot tell you everything you may want to know. This is why we tell you what leaflets to get if you want more detailed information. You can get

these leaflets free of charge from any Social Security office. Or you can write for them to the following address, telling them the leaflet titles and reference numbers of the ones you want:

ISCO5 (DSS),
The Paddock,
Frizinghall,
Bradford,
Yorkshire
BD9 4HD

And please remember:

- this is your own Retirement Pension Forecast. It does not include any Retirement Pension that your wife may be entitled to.
- a form inviting you to claim your State Retirement Pension will be sent to you automatically four months before you reach 65. So it is very important that you tell your local Social Security office if you change the address you gave us on your Forecast application form. But if for some reason you do not get a claim form before you are 65, please go to your local Social Security office without delay for advice.
- you cannot start getting Retirement Pension until you are 65, and have made a proper claim. And remember, you can still get Retirement Pension even if you go on working after you are 65.
- your Forecast has been worked out assuming that the information you gave us on your application form will not change. So if any of the information does change, or the rules about Retirement Pension are altered, then your future entitlement may be different.
- you should keep this letter in a safe place, together with any other information you may get from the

Department of Social Security. This is in case you have any queries when you eventually claim your State Retirement Pension.

If you need any more help or advice about your Retirement Pension Forecast, please take this letter NOW to your local Social Security office. The address is in the 'phone book under "Social Security" or "Health and Social Security". Or, if you would rather contact them in writing or by 'phone, please tell them the reference number shown at the top of this letter.

Yours sincerely,

APPENDIX TWO: BENEFIT LIMITS FOR EXECUTIVE PENSON SCHEMES

Unfortunately, no description of the benefit limits is going to be straightforward, because various recent budgets have changed the rules quite a lot. As they cannot change most pension scheme rules retrospectively, all their rule changes are for schemes set up after the budget in any particular year. This means we end up with a series of rules applying to various schemes depending on the date they were approved.

The principal recent changes concern:

- Length of service needed to qualify for a full pension
- The amount of pensionable earnings that can be taken into account
- The amount you can draw as a tax-free sum

To start from scratch – any executive pension plan set up on or after 17 March 1987: these new executive pension plans can provide a pension based on straight 60ths, for example, after eight years service you qualify for a pension of 8/60ths of your final salary. However, the company may offer an accelerated scale where higher benefits accrue. In this case it may be necessary for you to take into account any 'retained benefits' from past pension schemes. You can build up a two-thirds pension after ten years' service.

For an executive pension plan, post-March 1987, a two-thirds pension can be provided only if your total service will have been at least twenty years. If you put in less than that, then the maximum pension that may be paid is 1/30th for each year. If you joined an existing scheme between 16 March 1987 and 30 June 1987, then you will fall under the pre-17 March 1987 regime. The complete position is:

Table N: **Maximum pension payable under executive pension plans (and final salary schemes)**

Years of service to normal retirement age	Maximum fraction of final salary payable as pension	
	pre–17.3.1987	post–17.3.1987
1	1/60	2/60
2	2/60	4/60
3	3/60	6/60
4	4/60	8/60
5	5/60	10/60
6	8/60	12/60
7	16/60	14/60
8	24/60	16/60
9	32/60	18/60
10	40/60	20/60
11	40/60	22/60
12	40/60	24/60
13	40/60	26/60
14	40/60	28/60
15	40/60	30/60
16	40/60	32/60

17	40/60	34/60
18	40/60	36/60
19	40/60	38/60
20	40/60	40/60

On either scale, interpolation for part years is usually allowed. For example, under a new scheme, if there is going to be eleven years and three months' service, a pension of 22.5/60ths is usually acceptable.

Lump sum
At retirement, part of the pension can be taken as a tax-free sum. Under current legislation, that is worth doing because you can use the cash to buy a life annuity where part of each payment will itself be tax free (see Chapter Seven). In contrast, if you draw a pension direct, this is taxable as earned income.

For an executive pension plan set up on after 14 March 1989, the maximum permissible lump sum is the greater of:

● A fraction of 3/80ths of final salary times the number of years' service
● 2.25 times the pension being provided before it was commuted

Example 1:
Final salary of £48,000, ten years' service, no retained benefits from previous employers. The maximum pension is £16,000 (20/60ths of £48,000). The maximum lump sum is the greater of:

● 30/80ths of £48,000, i.e. £18,000, and
● 2.25 times £16,000, i.e. £36,000

So the maximum cash is £36,000.

For an executive pension plan set up before 17 March 1987, the maximum cash sum is given by the following table:

Table P: Maximum lump sum payable under executive pension plans (and final salary schemes) pre-17 March 1987

Years of service to normal retirement age	Maximum fraction of final salary payable as a lump sum
1	3/80
2	6/80
3	9/80
4	12/80
5	15/80
6	18/80
7	21/80
8	24/80
9	30/80
10	36/80
11	42/80
12	48/80
13	54/80
14	63/80
15	72/80
16	81/80
17	90/80
18	99/80
19	108/80
20	120/80

Interpolation of part-years is usually allowed.

For an executive pension plan set up in the period 17 March 1987 to 13 March 1989 inclusive, although the above table still applies, there is a further restriction. The cash can only be increased above 3/80ths for each year of service if the pension before commutation is above 1/60th for each year of service to the same extent.

Remember: any cash obtained by commutation of part of a pension must mean, obviously, that the pension is lower.

One final point which is worth noting is that any pension produced from an employee's voluntary contributions (AVCs) begun on or after 8 April 1987 must be taken as income.

Death before retirement
An approved executive pension plan may provide additional benefits:

- A cash lump sum of up to four times salary plus a return of the employee's contributions with interest
- A widow/er's pension of two-thirds of the member's prospective pension, expressed as a fraction, for example 4/9ths of salary if prospective total service was at least twenty years (ten years if the plan was set up before 17 March 1987)

On death after retirement
An executive pension plan may provide a widow/er's pension of up to two-thirds of the maximum approvable member's pension, for example 4/9ths of final salary if total service was at least twenty years (ten years if the plan was set up before 17 March 1987), whether or not that maximum pension was actually provided.

Example:
You retire after twenty years' service on a final salary of

£30,000 a year. The actual fund from your executive pension plan is not enough to get you a £20,000 pension, but it is enough to get you a £9,000 pension and a widow's pension of £9,000 if she survives you.

Cost of living increases
A pension which is being paid, whether at retirement or otherwise, may have cost of living increases built into it, within prescribed limits. In the absence of any special complications, the position is that the actual pension in payment must at no time exceed the maximum approvable initial pension increased by the greater of 3% a year or the increase in the Retail Prices Index. The same increases may be given on a spouse's pension.

Final salary
For the purposes of calculating your pension, your final salary is normally defined as:

● The salary paid for any one of the five years before retirement, subject to averaging out any fluctuations, usually over three years, or
● The average salary of any three consecutive years ending in the last ten

For certain directors, broadly those who directly or indirectly control 20% or more of the voting shares in the company employing them, only the latter definition is allowed.

For 'death-in-service' benefits, you can use any one of three definitions. The same as the ones for retirement benefits, the rate of salary paid at the date of death (subject to averaging fluctuating emoluments, usually over three years), or the total earnings of any one year ending not earlier than three years prior to death. If however, the executive pension plan was set up on or after 17 March 1987 and before 14 March 1989 an upper limit of £100,000 salary applies for calculating the lump sum, but see below. For retirement on or after that date, subject to transitional arrangements, anyone earning that amount, or more (as well as directors with a 20% stake) must use the three-year average definition.

Where the executive pension plan is set up on or after 14 March 1989, there is a harsher restriction in the form of an earnings cap. The figures to date are:

	Salary	Maximum Pension
1989–90	£60,000	£40,000
1990–91	£64,800	£43,200
1991–92	£71,400	£47,600

That is the upper limit of the definition of salary that can be taken into account. It is intended that this pensions cap will be increased annually in line with any increase in the Retail Prices Index.

Retirement date
The normal retirement date specified in the rules governing the executive pension scheme should be when the employee is actually expected to retire. Usually it should be no earlier than age sixty and no later than seventy-five.

Approvable contributions
The maximum total contribution, from employer and employee, is calculated by reference to the so-called maximum 'approvable benefits'. This means that total contributions should be sufficient to produce a pension of approved size but not excessive. While the employee cannot contribute more than 15% of his normal earnings, there is no restriction on the maximum employer's contribution. If large contributions are made by the employer to build up the fund quickly at the start, then

the company may not be able to offset some of them against profits in the same tax year, but may need to spread them forward.

In such a short description of a complex area of pension planning, it is impossible to cover every aspect. If you are considering setting up an approved executive pension plan, then you should talk to a financial adviser.

GLOSSARY

Accrual rate
The rate at which your pension builds up in a final earnings or average earnings scheme each year, usually expressed either as a fraction or a decimal. Many people are in 1/80th pension schemes; for each year they are members of the scheme, they receive 1/80th of their final pensionable earnings when they retire as a pension. After forty years, they would get 40/80ths, which is half their earnings. A better scheme would be a 1/60th pension scheme, giving 40/60ths or two-thirds after a full working life.

Actuarial surplus
The actuary is in effect drawing up a long-term budget for the pension scheme, to see what contribution is needed over future years. This is called a valuation. If the contributions being paid are going to produce more than is needed to pay the promised benefits, the scheme is said to be in surplus. If less, it is in deficit.

Actuary
The expert who calculates the contributions needed to pay the pensions that have been promised. Actuaries are mathematicians and their work involves using assumptions about probable life expectancy and investment

returns for many years into the future. The Government Actuary is a senior civil servant, with a small department of his own, who does the forecasting for state and public sector pension schemes.

Added years
People in public sector pension schemes and in some private ones can make extra contributions to buy themselves extra years' pension in the scheme, within certain limits. This can prove a cost-effective way of providing extra pension for yourself.

Additional pension (or component)
This is the earnings related element of the state scheme known as the State Earnings Related Pension Scheme (SERPS) paid on top of the basic pension which was introduced in 1978. The Department of Social Security works out the additional pension by taking your earnings between the Lower and Upper Earnings Levels and recalculating them to take account of the increase in national average earnings between the date you earned the money and your retirement. So, for instance, if you earned £100 a week in 1986–87 but by the time you retired earnings had doubled, they would recalculate this figure as £200. Having got a list of all these earnings figures for each year since 1978, they then average them and pay you 1/80th of that average figure for each year since then. The maximum you can get is 20/80ths or a quarter. So people retiring now, who have been in SERPS from the start, get 13/80ths of this figure, called their 'revalued average earnings', on top of their basic pension.

The government is reducing the amount that is available from SERPS, but this will not affect anyone in the state scheme directly until 1998.

Additional voluntary contributions (AVCs)
With any type of occupational pension scheme the employer must also make arrangements for members to make additional voluntary contributions, which are usually referred to by their initials as AVCs. Due to the favourable tax position, this is a very good way of saving, although rather inflexible. Once the contributions are paid, they normally have to remain invested in the scheme until you reach retirement date. You can only transfer them if you transfer the main scheme benefits too. You also have to take your benefits from both parts at the same time. All employers operating pension schemes have to make AVC facilities available to members. Alternatively, you can make your own private arrangements through a plan of your choice, known as a Freestanding AVC (FSAVC).

Age allowance
This special allowance replaces the personal allowance for both married and single people. For 1991–92 the personal age allowance is £4,020 (single), £6,375 (married couple) for people aged sixty-five to seventy-four. It goes up at age seventy-five. However, if your income exceeds £13,500, the age allowance is reduced.

Annuity
When someone retires, the lump sum that has built up in their pension fund is used to buy an annuity. The provider, an insurance company, agrees to pay a regular sum throughout your lifetime. The amount is based on factors such as the rate of investment returns expected in the accumulated fund and your age. Some annuities give a percentage increase each year, whilst others pay the same sum every year. Each insurance company applies its own assumptions in arriving at a rate for each type of annuity it offers. There can be quite large differences

between companies and between annuity rates at different times, depending on the level of interest rates. See also: Substituted annuities and Open market options.

Benefit statements
The statement most employers give which shows how much you have earned in the pension scheme to date. Since 1987, there has been a legal requirement to give you details of your pension entitlement.

Bonus
The amount added by an insurance company to the guaranteed sum in a with-profits policy, depending on how well their investments do. There are two main types. Reversionary bonuses are declared each year and added to the policy at the time. Terminal bonuses are added at the end of the policy term if the investment performance over the whole term of the policy warrants payment. Terminal bonuses are not guaranteed and should not be included in any calculations you make when trying to decide which is likely to be the best policy for you.

Commutation
When you retire, you can turn part of your pension into a lump sum, which is tax free, and this is called commuting it. For someone in an employer's pension scheme, the Inland Revenue applies limits of up to one and a half times your final earnings as a lump sum. Under self-employed policies effected before 1 July 1988 you may not take a sum more than three times the size of the pension that is left. Under personal pension schemes introduced from 1 July 1988, the amount you may take as a lump sum will simply be 25% of the fund that has built up for your benefit less any part of the fund which consists of contributions arising from contracting-out of SERPS. Usually, a man of sixty-five has to give up about

£1 of his annual pension to receive a £9 lump sum, while a woman of sixty giving up the same amount would receive £11, although these rates vary between schemes. In the public sector, the lump sum is generally paid automatically without any need to commute.

Contracting-out
If your employer's pension scheme gives a pension at least as good as the state additional pension the employer can contract-out of the state earnings related pension. The employer must guarantee to pay as much as you would have had from the state as pension, and this amount is called the Guaranteed Minimum Pension. In return for this, both you and your employer pay lower National Insurance contributions. Money purchase employer's schemes and personal pensions can also contract-out if the minimum contribution, equal to the National Insurance rebate and any incentive payments, is paid to them.

Deferral
If you leave your employment, the pension that is looked after for you to be collected when you retire is known as deferred or preserved pension.

Deferred annuity
This is an annuity which you buy well before retirement date and is paid when you retire.

Early leavers
Anyone who leaves a pension scheme when they are too young to take a pension immediately is classed as an early leaver, so this can in fact include people who have been members for twenty or thirty years. The Social Security Act 1985 says that people who become early leavers after January 1986 must have their pensions

inflation-proofed to some extent. The 1990 Social Security Act increases these requirements.

Final salary scheme
This is the main type of company pension scheme in this country at the present time. It means that the pension you are promised, in return for your contributions today, will be a proportion of your earnings at or near retirement. What proportion you receive will depend on the terms of your pension and the number of years you have been in the scheme. Sometimes the earnings used in the calculation are those in your last year before retirement. More often, an average is taken of the last three years, or your three years' top earnings out of the last ten.

Guaranteed Minimum Contribution
The minimum contribution paid to a money purchase scheme, either occupational or personal pension, to enable it to contract-out. It is equal to the National Insurance rebate and any incentive payments.

Guaranteed Minimum Pension
If your company is contracted-out of the State Earnings Related Pension Scheme using a final salary scheme, then it has to guarantee to pay you a certain amount of pension known, not surprisingly, as the Guaranteed Minimum Pension. The Department of Social Security will inform your company how much is due to you when you reach retirement.

Income tax
A tax due on earned and unearned income received by United Kingdom residents.

Integration
This is when a deduction is made from your occupational

pension to take account of the fact that you are also receiving a state pension and there are two methods of doing the calculation. One is to subtract from your earnings figure an amount usually equal to either 100% or 150% of the state pension. The other way is to deduct a proportion of the pension itself. The method used depends on the design of the scheme and will be decided when its terms are being drawn up by the employer or a consultant, often (but not always) in consultation with the members.

Loanback

This is an arrangement, available in some self-employed plans and those for executives, under which you can borrow a sum related to the value of the fund built up for you. The amount you can borrow is usually linked to the size of the pension fund being accumulated on your behalf. Sometimes, instead, it is a multiple of your contributions. The lender will often require that you put all or most of the money into a guaranteed fund, rather than a unit-linked one which can go up or down with the value of the stock market. Interest rates and the terms of the loan will vary between lenders. Your tax position on such a loan is the same as if it came from any other source, but you will be benefiting meanwhile from the special tax advantages of pension schemes.

Lower Earnings Level

This is set by the government each year and is roughly linked to the state basic pension. In 1991–92 it is £52 per week. You pay National Insurance contributions only if you earn more than this in a week. The additional pension is based on earnings above this level. (See also, Upper Earnings Level.)

Money purchase

This is a pension plan where the size of contributions, rather than the benefits, are stated. You and perhaps also your employer pay a specified amount. The managers will invest the contributions to try and build up the largest possible fund. All profits, dividends and interest are rolled up tax free inside the fund. By the time you retire a lump sum will have been built up which will then be used to buy you an annuity. The size of your pension will depend on how well your money has been invested, the level of running expenses and what the annuity rates are at the time you retire. As all these factors vary widely, people retiring after the same number of years' service and on the same wage could end up with very different pensions. These could be much higher than under the alternative final earnings schemes, where benefits are fixed in advance, or much lower. Much depends on the investment environment overall as well as the individual manager's expertise. The new breed of personal pensions introduced in 1988 is of this type.

National Insurance contributions

The contributions all employees and self-employed people pay to qualify for both a pension and other state benefits. How much you pay depends on your earnings. If you earn less than the Lower Earnings Level you pay no contributions. However, as soon as you earn above this level, you pay contributions on your earnings up to the Upper Earnings Level at the same rate. The rate you pay varies according to whether you are contracted-in or out of the State Earnings Related Pension Scheme and according to the level of your earnings.

Occupational Pensions Board

The government body, set up in 1973, which supervises some areas of occupational pensions. It covers areas such as equal access for men and women, contracting-out and early leavers' benefits.

Open market options
Insurance companies must offer these. It means that you are entitled to shop around and obtain the best annuity rate when you retire even if this means switching companies. You should check a policy before taking it out to make sure this option is included. An open market option gives you the chance when you retire to study the market in what are called 'substituted annuities', though you will find it no more expensive and well worth while to ask a broker or a firm of benefit consultants to do the donkey-work for you. The company your plan is with then has to transfer your money direct to the new company, who will pay you an annuity for life.

Pension mortage
This is an arrangement under which you can use the lump sum you will receive from your pension scheme at retirement to pay off your mortgage. It can be a very tax-efficient method of paying for your mortgage, but do make sure you contribute enough to also provide your-self with a reasonable pension. It means you decide in advance what you will be doing with the tax-free lump sum, even if at retirement you might prefer (or need) to use it for something else.

Permanent health insurance
This is a way of covering long term sickness. Permanent health insurance (PHI) is also called disability insurance, but should not be confused with private medical insur-ance. It can be taken out by individuals or employers. The benefits are related to the size of your wages. The aim is that the insurance payments when added to any state benefits due will make up any income shortfall you

experience through being unable to work due to an extended illness.

Usually the policy will make up your earnings to two-thirds of what they would have been, subject to an overall limit of 75% when the PHI and social security benefits are added together. If any employer takes out one of these policies for the workforce, there will normally be Corporation Tax relief on the cost, but an individual who takes out a policy does not get tax relief. Individuals who take out policies will usually have to pass a medical. It's possible and well worthwhile to take out a policy which carries on paying the pension contributions while you are off sick.

Personal pensions
This term can be used to mean two different things. Firstly, it can cover pensions taken out by the self-employed and those not in an employer's pension scheme under the old legislation prior to July 1988. Secondly, it is the name for the plans introduced in the summer of 1988 by the Thatcher government. You can use these new personal pensions to opt out of SERPS and have an individual policy issued in your own name rather than having to remain in your company's scheme.

Protected rights
Where a money purchase arrangement is contracted-out, the contributions which are paid as a result of contracting-out make up Protected Rights. There are restrictions on the type of benefits which the Protected Rights fund is used to buy.

Revalued average earnings
See: Additional pension

Section 32 buy-out
This is an insurance company policy which you buy with

the money built up in a pension scheme after you have left it and which is used to give you a pension when you retire. This type of policy was first introduced by Section 32 of the Finance Act 1981.

Section 226
This was a personal pension policy for self-employed people and those not in a pension scheme run by their employers and was available until 30 June 1988.

Section 226A policy
This was the life assurance policy that the self-employed and those employees not in an occupational pension plan could take out in conjunction with their Section 226 pension policy. The legislation setting out the rules formed Section 226A of the Income and Corporation Taxes Act 1970. You receive full tax relief on your contributions, up to 5% of your net relevant earnings.

SERPS
The State Earnings Related Pension Scheme, brought in by Barbara Castle of the then Labour government as part of the Social Security Act in 1975. SERPS pensions started building up in 1978. The scheme provides not only a pension after retirement but also widows' and widowers' benefits, invalidity benefits and 'home responsibility protection' for people looking after children and invalids at home.

State earnings related pension
See: Additional pension and SERPS.

Substituted annuities
Most pension plans now give you the option of shopping around for the best annuity rates on retirement. When you take advantage of this flexibility you are purchasing

a substituted annuity.

Superannuation
The word used in the civil service and other public services for occupational pensions.

Superannuation Funds Office
The section of the Inland Revenue that deals exclusively with pension schemes, with the responsibility for seeing that the Finance Acts and the practice notes are properly enforced and checking pension schemes to ensure that they should be granted 'tax approval'.

Surplus
See: Actuarial surplus

Tax approval
In order to be granted approval and so enjoy all the tax benefits available, a pension scheme must meet the various Inland Revenue requirements.

Transfer value
The cash value of the pension you build up in one scheme and then transfer to another scheme or company, or personal pension or buy-out bond. This is calculated by an actuary on the basis of the likely value of your rights when you retire, following guidelines laid down by the Institute of Actuaries. For money purchase, it is the value of your fund. The transfer value must then be paid to the organisation which is going to provide your pension. It cannot be paid direct into your hands.

Trustees
Trustees of a pension fund have a legal duty to act in the best interest of the beneficiaries, not according to their own wishes. Many schemes have trustees chosen from

among its members, but there is no legal right to this.

Upper Earnings Level
For 1991–92 this is £390 a week. You do not pay National Insurance contributions or earn a state pension on earnings above this limit. (See also, Lower Earnings Level.)

Waiver of contributions
This is an option, under many personal pensions, to pay an extra premium to cover any gaps in your earnings power due to illness or injury. The insurance company will then fill in the gaps, for as long as you are sick, so that you do not lose pension in the end. The upper age limit is usually fifty-five and the cost is about 3% of premiums or more if you are in a dangerous occupation or the insurance company decides that you are more likely to fall ill than the average applicant.

Working life
The number of years counted by the Department of Social Security when they calculate your basic pension. To qualify for a full basic pension, you must have paid or been credited with National Insurance contributions for about 9/10ths of your working life. For most people, this starts at the age of sixteen, even if you left school earlier. There are special arrangements for students.